EATABILITY

JOCASTA INNES
EATABILITY
WITH BRONWEN CUNNINGHAM

A fresh approach to easy food from the author of 'The Pauper's Cookbook'

Macdonald Orbis

A Macdonald Orbis BOOK

Text copyright © Jocasta Innes and Bronwen Cunningham 1987
Illustrations copyright © Macdonald & Co (Publishers) Ltd 1987

First published in Great Britain in 1987
by Macdonald & Co (Publishers) Ltd
London & Sydney

A member of BPCC plc

British Library Cataloguing in Publication Data

Innes, Jocasta
Eatability.
1. Cookery, International
I. Title
641.5   TX725.A1
ISBN 0-356-14720-7

Typeset by Tradespools, Frome

Printed and bound in Italy by OFSA SpA

Illustrations by Lisa Adamczewski

Editor: Gillian Prince
Art Editor: Simon Webb
Designer: Annie Tomlin

Macdonald & Co (Publishers) Ltd
Greater London House
Hampstead Road
London NW1 7QX

CONTENTS

INTRODUCTION

I have met very few people, perhaps half a dozen, who struck me as being natural born cooks, with that mysterious intelligence in their hands which seems to coax the best performance from any ingredients under all circumstances. Most good cooks are not born but made, or rather self-made through intelligent study of cookbooks and much practice and experiment. The other attribute necessary to good cooking, in my view, is healthy greed.

Healthy, or creative, greed differs from gluttony in being a sociable, generously disposed vice, if indeed an instinct which generates so much harmless pleasure can be called a vice at all. Non-greedy people can become skilled cooks at a mechanical level, reproducing dishes reliably and well, but creative greed is what lures one on into trying to do better and different, into such culinary adventures as boning ducks, pickling pork, stuffing sausage skins, crunching off on frosty mornings in search of wild fungi, lacerating fingers to fill a basket of wild blackberries, sitting up till the small hours monitoring the raised pie whose juices simply will not run clear. Little adventures like these can end in tears or embarrassment (try bringing a whole garlic sausage in your handluggage on your next flight home from abroad), but they keep cooking real and challenging in the teeth of so much that is designed to make it as easy, and boring, as ordering the week's groceries by computer. Cooking, at least some of the time, is a creative activity, for some people their most creative activity, and as with any other form of creativity the moment it all begins to come too pat and easy the likelihood is you are losing your touch.

Now that most women everywhere are out at work a good deal of their lives, the old idea that children learnt to cook by watching or helping their mother, or grandmother, has pretty much gone by the board. Instead, our mentors are cookery writers, which is no bad thing if you choose your mentors wisely, follow their injunctions scrupulously the first time round, and then feel free to kick over the traces. The good cookery writer, like the wise parent, provides guidelines and rules and may even unobtrusively form developing taste, but only to the point where you feel emboldened to set up on your own, making mayonnaise in a processor, using basil where the mentor recommends tarragon, and generally asserting your right to do your own thing.

In other words, use recipes but don't let them run your life. This may sound obvious to some, but it is surprisingly easy to be cowed by precedent and bullied by recipes. How many people, looking down a list of ingredients and finding that they lack some, even only one or two, will discard it as impracticable and move on? OK, so you can't reasonably make chicken Kiev without chicken, but you can, for instance, make bread without flour but with ground chick peas, or with barley, and you can make burgers of a sort without meat. All I'm getting at is that recipes should not be regarded as final and inviolable. Traditional recipes one tampers with less, perhaps, because most of them have already been whittled by time and use into a formula so spare, and refined, that altering or removing one element ruins the dish. Then there are recipes which have something of the inflexibility of chemical formulae: you won't cause an explosion if you subtract eggs from a soufflé, or bake a cake at half the prescribed heat, but you will have a soufflé like a washrag and a cake like sticky porridge. Most recipes, however, whatever the pedants and pundits may claim, are not so fixed that a new generation of chefs can't come along and re-invent them.

We all need recipes the first time of trying a new or unfamiliar dish, or technique, and beginners will have to refer back to the book for as long as it takes for a set of learned instructions and quantities to become second nature. But don't let foodism get you down: it isn't a sin to curdle a mayonnaise or cook pasta to a glutinous lump. We all learned by making mistakes. Let your creative greed bounce back. Try again, and move on. The day will come when you can do it without looking at the book, subtracting and adding ingredients as inspiration and the larder dictate, and it comes out perfect, a dream, and all your friends cry out for second and third helpings. That is a good moment, to be treasured and offset against the red-faced ones when the eagerly awaited pâté maison leaks gore on to the plate, or the steaming paella is like eating mouthfuls of lead shot.

Cooking is mysteriously subjective. Some days you can't do a thing wrong, others the bio-rhythms play up and everything backfires. Looked at philosophically, as Brillat Savarin advises us to do, the capacity to make mistakes is one of the things that distinguishes us from the animal creation, and the capacity to learn from our mistakes and keep trying to do better is what ultimately makes a blundering novice into a good and confident cook.

FIRST PRINCIPLES

There is more to food than following recipes, and good cooks agree that the quality of the ingredients is as important as the way they are cooked. I gravitate towards fresh seasonal foods all the year round and apart from a few staples keep very little in the way of convenience foods: a few cans and perhaps some instant coffee. Buying and cooking fresh ingredients is more enjoyable and takes little longer than deciphering the small print on processed and prepacked foods. In my book the only good additives are the harmless traditional ones — the spices, herbs and seasonings that every well-dressed kitchen should feature. This "nuts and bolts" chapter looks at intelligent shopping, and offers a brief glimpse into a healthily-stocked store cupboard. Part of the secret of preparing wholesome fresh food effortlessly lies in having the right equipment, so I've begun by setting the scene in the kitchen.

THE WELL-TEMPERED KITCHEN: EQUIPMENT

The most lavishly equipped kitchen does not always produce the best food; indeed, there is a cut-off point beyond which technology just seems to get in the way. Having said that, there are some investments one never regrets as well as some items — not necessarily expensive — one can't imagine being able to do without. For me, a swivel-bladed **vegetable peeler** I picked up in a street market for next to nothing is a jewel of functional design, a treasure I reach for to pare carrots, turnips and all the other homely roots that feature increasingly in my household's meals. Nothing else performs this job so well — not even the razor-like French and Swiss steel **knives** with riveted handles which I collect in a wide variety of shapes and sizes, and value above any gadget ever invented. I keep them well sharpened and use them for shredding vegetables and slicing potatoes in preference to the shredding attachment on my food processor, not just because it takes no longer as a rule but because I actually enjoy the sensation of wielding a keen blade efficiently. Everyone should have a selection of the best available of these — ranging upwards from a little pointed vegetable knife to a substantial cook's knife for cutting meat — kept on a magnetic rack near to the relevant worktop.

I am fond of my ageing **food processor** (which has to be propped up where a foot has gone missing, and bodily restrained from hopping about as it gets up speed!), and use it daily for reducing fresh bread to crumbs, for grating cheese quickly, for pulverizing herbs and grinding raw and cooked meat. On balance, though, I would trade it in for a set of superlative **copper-bottomed stainless steel pans**, with lids that really hug the pan, handles and knobs that do not heat up agonizingly (an astonishingly common design fault) and with steamers *en suite* to put an end forever to fiddly improvisation with dangling sieves. Having experimented with boiling hams in the strangest assortment of containers, never adequately capacious, I would dearly love a purpose-made lidded pan in the same range, which would cost as much (alas!) as a short trip abroad. There is real aesthetic pleasure in handling pans of Rolls-Royce quality: three — small, medium and large — would be a better investment than the most lavish and expensive dinner service.

Enamelled iron cooking pots, with lids, are the best for oven cookery, in my experience, and a **non-stick frying pan** or two in the same range seems to produce the most even heat and controllable frying. Treated with respect (never scour, or use abrasive powder), these gradually acquire a patina which replaces the slowly eroded non-stick finish and is just as effective.

Two sensible gadgets any kitchen could use are a spinning-top **salad drier** made of plastic, and a **cordless jug kettle** which saves hours of plugging and unplugging to reach the sink as well as being much easier to fill via the spout than the average kettle, an eccentricity almost everyone I know is guilty of. A well-designed four-square **grater**, steel or plastic, saves scraped knuckles.

Some people must have a **liquidizer**; certainly a basic blender is wonderful for making soups and sauces creamy. But if you don't mind — or actually prefer — soups with identifiable contents, there is no necessity for a liquidizer, which can make almost anything into a homogeneous mass of indeterminate colour. It's the kitchen equivalent of the mechanical hedge-cutter, reducing a tree to fine splinters in a twinkling. Back to lumps? Not really, but it is nice to know what you are eating sometimes. A **potato-masher** comes in handy for smoothing soups a little but not totally.

No one can have too many **wooden spoons**, with long as well as short handles, but a **wooden fork** is gentler with rice and other grains and cereals than a spoon. Since my rotary egg-beater disintegrated I use a **wire whisk** and kitchen bowl to beat eggs, cream etc, but though just as effective this does take longer. A small **jug** with a pinched-up beak is invaluable for leaking oil a drop at a time into the mayonnaise. One also needs **wire sieves** and **strainers**, **colanders**, a **rolling pin** and large efficient **kitchen scissors**. Rather than fluted china flan dishes which are less efficient than tin, spend the money on small china **ramekins** with a multitude of uses.

A capacious transparent **measuring jug** or set of **cups** is essential, preferably marked with volume equivalents for different ingredients so that you can dispense with a weighing machine for most things. You also need nests of plastic **measuring spoons** for smaller amounts, unless you know by heart the sizes of particular spoons of your own.

If you have to equip on a tight budget, start small and buy the best you can afford. One excellent pan, with lid, is worth a whole set of dinky lightweight pans however coppery and cute (you will never clean them), and learning to make one pan do the work of several is useful training – in lateral thinking, among other things. If you really can afford only one pan, let it be a **wok**, the best available, with a lid. It can be used for boiling and steaming as well as stir-frying.

The greatest argument for the minimalist approach is that another commodity in short supply in most kitchens is space. Clear surfaces and organized storage magically concentrate the mind while clutter and inessentials merely confuse it.

So you're equipped with stove, sink and refrigerator. You need cupboard space for storage – but beware packets stamped "Best before end 1962" that lurk at the back of too-deep shelves. You also need surface space. At some point you've got a blazing hot dish in one hand burning through the holes in the oven-cloth: you desperately make a corner by balancing a nearby bowl on top of an already tottering pile of plates... What saves the day in my house is a pull-out shelf made of blockboard or thick ply, the width of one cupboard, just below the working surface. I once inherited two in an ancient sink fitting, and now incorporate the idea in every move and change: I

have one just to the right of the stove, to use for chopping, for resting things on when they come out of the oven, and as an overflow at all times. The secret of its success is that it *has* to be cleared because it is pushed away. And it doesn't matter if the surface gets burnt or scratched.

SKILFUL SHOPPING

Shopping becomes much less of a chore if you become skilful at it. One element of skill is being able to recognize quality; another is to allow some flexibility to invade your tidy list so that seasonal bargains or delicacies – or both – can be substituted on impulse without hassle or guilt. Experienced shoppers and cooks leave room for manoeuvre, letting the food available suggest the dishes rather than planning the dishes and then hunting for the necessary ingredients.

The best supermarkets are hard to beat in the range and value of the food they offer, but there is a sameness about most of the fish and meat that makes me prefer to go to specialist fishmongers and butchers whenever I have the time. Not only is their range wider, with all sorts of things ignored by supermarkets that have their place in the stocks, soups and sauces of a lively diet, but the quality is noticeably better, too. The good tradesman will advise you reliably, as well as doing fiddly things – like plucking, boning or filleting, and small favours – like finding you recherché items such as sausage skins. Relationships like these humanize shopping, as well as stimulating the cook.

I always buy local produce whenever I get the chance, whether it is bags of earthy potatoes from a roadside stall or knobbly green tomatoes at a garden fête. Usually these work out cheaper; often they taste indescribably better than store-bought goods, but finally it is the element of uncertainty, non-standardization, that makes them so attractive. Freshness has a pungent flavour which is all the more precious if one lives and shops and eats in a big city, and is well worth making a detour along secondary roads to find. Markets, too, are a good bet when shopping for fruit and vegetables, because their turnover tends to be fast so the food is fresher; in country areas much of the produce may even be locally grown.

FISH

Fish is the darling of modern chefs and nutritionists alike. The only obstacles to its becoming the single most popular form of animal protein must be its cost, plus the sad fact that it is still not possible to buy really fresh and interestingly varied fish everywhere. Once people discover what excellent eating fresh fish really is (as well as being healthy in all the ways dieticians keep pointing out), perhaps they will start campaigning for a better-quality product and fishmongers will have to look lively; meantime, if you are lucky enough to have an enterprising and conscientious wet fish supplier in your neighbourhood, you will be doing yourself and everyone else a good turn by becoming a regular and choosy customer.

Fishmongers are dedicated souls, willing to give advice on buying, preparing and even cooking; they are ready to decapitate, clean, bone and fillet fish if you don't catch them with a long queue of customers. (If you insist on keeping the trimmings, you will have the basis of stock for making some of the most dazzling, delicate soups ever devised.) So the first rule is always to ask — if you're not sure what amount to buy, or can't identify a strange-looking fish, or don't known what to do with it.

There's a missionary zeal, usually, in fish shops. Anyone can buy and sell meat, but it takes an independent and enquiring spirit to deal in fish in a country where people are full of absurd fears: they are afraid of choking on bones, of stinking the kitchen out, of fish ''going bad'' on them, even it seems of handling this alien slippery creature. Yet as anyone who has eaten the freshest fish knows, it is one of the most succulent, subtle, fastidious foods to be found, as comforting to the innards as

it is rewarding to the tastebuds, and a delight to cook because it combines so well with so many different styles and seasonings. Fish goes with bacon, surprisingly. Fresh ginger, grated. Artichokes — the Jerusalem kind. Fennel roots and leaves. Herb stuffings, especially marjoram and thyme. Savoury butters — *maître d'hôtel*, parsley, lemon and paprika, dill and mustard. Watercress is good with trout. Apple and gooseberry complement rich oily fish like herring and mackerel. So does oatmeal; mustard is good, too. And always something sharp: lemon, tomato, capers, olives, dry wine, orange, garlic . . .

Generally a clear bulging eye and firm-textured flesh — someone once said a fresh mackerel should be as firm and springy as a cucumber — are reliable indications of freshness. The problem is that once a fish is filleted or cut up these useful clues disappear, and many fishmongers have little in the way of whole fish on display. Buying a whole fish is the best guarantee of quality. You don't have to eat it at one sitting: there are lots of recipes — salads as well as fishcakes — which make use of left-over cooked fish.

For fish pies look for chunky white fish, with large easily-removed bones, or none at all (fillets or cutlets need no preparation). Choose coley, haddock, cod, hake, monkfish or huss; salmon is good, too. A mixture of different fish can be a good buy — half fresh white fish, and half smoked haddock or smoked cod to add extra flavour and texture.

For baking choose fillets of these chunky white fish, or cook whole fish such as bass, bream, mullet and trout. Prevent drying out by covering with a moist stuffing, sauce or vegetables, or wrapping in foil — or even in pastry.

For plain frying and **grilling/broiling**, the oily fish are the ones to choose: mackerel, herring, sardines, smelt, sprats and whitebait. The last two, if small, can be deep- or shallow-fried whole, and sardines need only topping and tailing. Meaty tuna steaks are excellent grilled/broiled or fried. Skate is usually cooked just as it comes, with generous amounts of browned butter and lemon or orange juice.

For stir-fried or cold **salad dishes**, choose a firm-textured fish that will not disintegrate easily (eg monkfish or huss), shellfish (eg scallops, shrimps, prawns, mussels, clams) or seafood (eg squid or calamari).

Smoked fish is often artificially coloured: look for paler fish, and ask if the colour is natural (avoid dark brown kippers and bright yellow cod or haddock). There's often little to choose between cod and haddock fillets: finnan haddock, on the bone, is best. Thin fillets of kipper tend to dry out: it's best to buy whole, plump, pale kippers. Cook in hot water or milk — or marinate. Choose smoked mackerel and trout with plump moist flesh that is not dried out. They are very filling — you need a smaller amount than of the unsmoked kind.

Prawns and shrimps taste much better bought in their shells, whether fresh or frozen. A few give a lift to an everyday fish dish.

All fish needs very little cooking and so is economical in time and energy.

The fresher it is, almost any fish is more delicious than you would expect.

Like meat, fish is full of high-grade protein, but unlike meat it's low in fat. Even the so-called oily fish like herring and mackerel contain only as much fat as chicken (far less than pork or lamb), and this is polyunsaturated and rich in vitamins and essential fatty acids.

MEAT

The British have always been enthusiastic meat eaters and the best British dishes are predominantly meaty — roast beef, of course, baked York and Bradenham hams, Wiltshire pork pies, stuffed chine and many more. One reason for this carnivorousness must be the famously high quality of the home-raised meat itself. Another could well be the climate: on damp chilly days people seem to require solid fuel, and nothing warms the belly so sustainingly as a few ounces of high-grade animal protein. My own cooking bears the imprint of this heritage: in spite of my fondness for stir-fries and satays, every so often the need comes upon me for a good old steak-and-kidney pudding or a carvable roast.

Here as everywhere, as meat becomes relatively more expensive, people are becoming ever more imaginative and adventurous in the way they cook and eat it. Instead of insisting that every meal must centre around a hunk of meat shored up with mounds of veg — a prejudice that did nothing for the standard of British cookery — the fact has finally got home that meat can play a supporting role in a dish with even more delicious and equally nourishing results. (Chinese cookery has always tended to use meat sparingly but with good effect.) Health and diet propaganda has reinforced the trend, making people at risk wary of overdoing the animal fats, hence the increasing popularity of lean cuts over fatty ones and of inherently lean meats like chicken, rabbit, venison and game generally. It may or may not be coincidental that these types of meat (apart from chicken — and free-range birds are becoming more widely available) are also more characterful and make better-flavoured eating than the standard shrink-wrapped supermarket offerings.

BEEF

The plainer and more classic the cooking method, the more tender and expensive the cut needs to be. **For roasting**, sirloin and fillet/tenderloin are best and most expensive; cuts from the rib are considerably cheaper and also good. **For pot-roasting** (in a covered pan with a little liquid), choose topside/top round or brisket. **For grilling/broiling** and **frying**, buy tender steak, cut in thick slices, or ask the butcher to recommend a cut. **For stewing**, buy skirt or chuck steak and remove any fat; shin/shank needs longest cooking and tends to be gelatinous but yields superlative gravy. **For pies** or **puddings**, buy braising steak, buttock/round steak or chuck. Butchers often do several grades of minced/ground beef, and it is worth spending more for a leaner quality, or getting some lean braising steak or skirt especially minced/ground.

Affinities with beef include root vegetables, particularly swedes/rutabaga, carrots, turnips, parsnips: roast them in the pan around the meat, serve as purées, or glazed with a little sugar and butter. Green vegetables such as cabbage, Brussels sprouts, calabrese and broccoli are good, too. Cook beef stews in beer, wine or fruit juice; add sesame oil and mace or thick slices of bread spread with mustard. All sorts of mustards and spicy relishes complement beef — horseradish, Worcestershire sauce, mushroom relish — as do garlic and shallots, separately, or all combined in a spicy concoction with a little vinegar and brown sugar.

LAMB

This ranges between succulent expensive home-produced and imported frozen (which can also be good, though not *as* good). Some fat may need trimming off before cooking. **For roasting**, choose saddle (a series of double loin chops), leg or shoulder (less expensive; fattier, but tasty), or stuffed breast. **For grilling/broiling** and **frying**, choose chump/shoulder or loin chops, or best end of neck cutlets/rib chops. **For stews** and **hotpots**, choose breast and scrag end/neck.

Affinities with lamb include flavours that balance the fattiness: aromatic herbs like rosemary, thyme and mint (but *not* mint sauce drowning in *malt* vinegar); sweet, pungent spices like coriander and cardamom; fruity sauces based on redcurrant, cranberry, orange; and garlic, of course. Most lamb benefits from being marinated (for even as little as half an hour) in wine or lemon juice.

PORK

Even lean pork is a fatty meat, though (as with lamb) the fattier cuts are often the best-tasting. Never undercook pork: cook until the juices run clear. **For roasting**, the leanest, priciest joints are loin and leg; cheaper are spare rib joints and hand/Boston and picnic shoulder cuts. **For casseroles** and **stews**, choose spare rib chops/shoulder blade steaks and lean belly/fresh side pork. For **stir-frying** and also **baking** (stuffed) in pastry, choose

fillet or tenderloin: expensive, but very versatile, and a little goes a long way.

Affinities with pork include tart apples in all guises: sauce, juice, crab apple jelly, sage and onion stuffing sharpened with apple. Some sweetness helps counteract pork's fat richness: sugar, honey, raisins with cinnamon, prunes stuffed with apple chutney, redcurrant jelly, pineapple — sliced, or juice — prunes, oranges, apricots. In sweet and sour sauces, cook pork with celery, bean sprouts, peanuts, and mushrooms.

CHICKEN

The flavour of fresh or chill-fresh rather than frozen birds is well worth the extra money: frozen chicken is mostly skin and water. Buying pieces is useful for specific dishes, but I always like to have the carcass (plus gizzard etc) for stock.

Affinities with chicken are infinite: herbs, especially tarragon, dill, rosemary; coriander, sesame, lemon, grapes, fragrant mustards; mushrooms, cream — flavours that complement chicken's mildness.

RABBIT

Buy fresh or imported frozen (soak overnight in acidulated water to whiten the meat and soften any strong taste).

Affinities with rabbit are similar to those for chicken. Cook in onion sauce, wine or cider to prevent drying out; cook on a bed of lettuce or cabbage, with apple juice, onions, mustard; serve with little balls of stuffing, rolls of bacon, and balls or cubes of puff pastry.

VEGETABLES

The more vegetables we all eat, the better we'll be. And the fresher the vegetable, the less tampered with, the better. As soon as a turnip is torn from the ground — or a lettuce cut off in its prime or a Brussels sprout nipped from its stem — it begins to lose nutrients. So look for fresh, firm skin and good colours in all vegetables. Always give them a good look-over, making sure that tomatoes aren't bruised and that onions are hard. Inspect the leaves at the top of a head of celery and those surrounding broccoli and cauliflower florets. Pea and bean pods should be fresh green and unwrinkled; mangetout (snow or sugar peas) should be crisp rather than limp. Stalks of chard or beet leaves should snap rather than bend.

Choose small vegetables where possible: they are usually tastiest and tenderest. Use them as soon as you can. Don't peel or chop them too far in advance, since they lose vitamins to the air and water. (There's no need to become paranoid, but it's a fact to bear in mind.) Stir-frying, steaming, or boiling in a very little water (which you can use later in soup) — for as short a time as you can — are the best ways to preserve the food value of vegetables. Microwaves and pressure-cookers score by cooking quickly, and in very little liquid.

Take the carrot. Small is best. The newest and tiniest can be just washed and eaten raw and whole: there's about twice as much vitamin A in raw carrots as in any other fruit or vegetable. Earthy carrots should be scrubbed — no need to peel. Don't buy washed carrots in plastic bags: the washing makes them deteriorate quickly and likely as not you'll find some mushy bits when you get them home. Or take the potato, an important source of vitamin C. Most of the nutrients are under the skin, so if you must peel them, cook first and peel later.

DAIRY PRODUCTS

It's generally acknowledged that we ought to eat less saturated or animal fats (found mostly in milk, cheese, cream, butter, eggs and meat, and also in hard margarines; they are the ones that contain cholesterol, which may cause heart trouble). We need some fat, but mustn't overdo it. Mono-unsaturated or polyunsaturated fats are found in most vegetable oils and contain no cholesterol, though processing can convert these polyunsaturates into saturates, as happens with hard margarine.

"Dairy" is a form of shorthand, of course: some of these products originate in the palm grove rather than the dairy farm.

BUTTER AND MARGARINE

Some hard margarines have just as much saturated fat as butter, so have no advantage from a health point of view. Inspect and read the labels of soft margarines carefully. Look for "vegetable oils and fats" among the ingredients — not just plain oil and fat. Buy unhydrogenated brands if possible. Watch out for added colour — yellow colouring can be harmful.

Use less butter where its special taste will not be missed, and where stronger flavours will eclipse it: a mixture of oil and butter for browning food, for instance; a mixture of margarine and butter in savoury butters pounded with herbs, garlic, anchovies and so on (not soft margarine here, or they won't set firm). Keep real butter for situations where its special flavour makes a genuine contribution: for tossing succulent steamed vegetables to serve with simply cooked meat, for example, or in delicate, fragrant petits fours to serve with home-made ice cream.

CREAMS, YOGURTS AND CHEESES

The supermarkets are stocking many varieties of low-fat cheeses and yogurts, and different kinds of cream and milk. It can be bewildering. If you are especially on the look-out for low fat, check the percentage *and* the calorie content: a high calorie count must mean high fat.

Crème fraîche is slightly soured rich cream, much used in France. *Fromage frais* and *fromage blanc* are lower in fat and useful for making dips and cold sauces. Smetana is another low-fat soured cream, a little like yogurt.

Yogurt can vary greatly in the amount of fat: most supermarkets do a low-fat version. "Strained" Greek yogurt is richest and creamiest (and most calorific), but also best for cooking. Like *fromage frais* it will separate when heated, so stabilize with 1 teaspoon cornflour/cornstarch or 1 egg per 300 ml/½ pint/1¼ cups yogurt.

Skimmed-milk soft cheeses are lowest in fat: 2% or less. Low-fat soft cheeses (including cottage cheeses and the German Quark) have 1–10% fat. Curd cheese is higher in fat. Full-fat cream cheeses contain at least 20% fat — often a lot more.

BEING PREPARED: THE STORE CUPBOARD

Even with all-night supermarkets and ethnic grocers keeping punishingly long hours, there will always be emergencies when a busy cook has to fall back on the store cupboard. It is powerfully calming to know that the supplies are there, varied enough to open up lots of possibilities from the ten-minute spaghetti carbonara for six teenagers to the cheer-up treat, on a cold miserable night, for one tired body. Besides the materials for creative improvisation, any good store cupboard — which may overflow into larder or fridge — should be primed with the non-perishable items, dry goods like rice, dried beans and peas etc which need frequent replenishing, plus all the interesting seasonings and flavourings that are vital to creative greed.

The main problem with a store cupboard, I find, is that out of sight means out of mind, and things run out unobserved. One way around this is to keep as much as possible in glass jars (but away from the light), which allows one to check at a glance. Another (if you are fairly sure of your supplier) is to buy non-perishable items in large quantities.

SPICES AND SEASONINGS

I invariably buy peppercorns, mustard seeds, cardamom pods, cumin and coriander from Asian grocers, a pound or so at a time. Arguably the flavour may fade slightly with time, but less than with the tiny drums of ground spices sold in most stores at inflated prices. I keep a lavish selection of spices, including unusual ones like fenugreek and poppy seeds, because I enjoy experimenting with them on plain vegetable dishes or in conventional stews and ragouts, as well as in authentic oriental dishes.

I buy Chinese spices from Chinese shops, saffron from a local Spanish deli, paprika, juniper berries and suchlike from foodie havens like the Harrods' food hall: it is worth paying more for something like paprika, because unless it is genuine and good, it is no more help to food than facepowder.

All **herbs** taste better fresh: basil, for instance, will grow in a pot on a windowsill. Herbs that dry acceptably include basil itself; keep some in the store cupboard, plus dried oregano, marjoram, dill and thyme. Dried bay leaves, too, are fine — essential for stews, fish, tomatoes.

One item I find myself taking much more seriously lately is **mustard**, the busy person's instant flavour-booster for spreading on meat or fish, thickening and zapping up sauces, adding to salad dressings. Again, I like to buy the best foreign import rather than supermarket own-label, and I succumb to any interesting variants — herb and fruit flavourings, and versions with alcohol.

Since we drink wine rather than spirits there is usually a bottle on the go for adding to suitable dishes. I like to keep white **vermouth** handy, too, because its astringency does a lot for simple impromptu meat or fish dishes which need a little sauce. Vermouth, like **sherry**, "lifts" flavours without being overpowering. But increasingly I find myself experimenting with non-alcoholic liquids, such as **fruit juices**, fresh or packaged. Apple is good with pork. Pineapple goes well with chicken stews ("What *is* this taste?" they ask). Fresh lime juice squeezed over plain fish, or meat, or a salad, makes a lot of difference for very little effort.

I keep **cider vinegar** and **wine vinegar** to use in salad dressings and sweet-sour dishes. A splash gives bite to meat dishes such as beef stews. Pickled **capers** have the same effect and do wonders for fish and tasteless chickens, as well as pizza toppings. Chopped **black** or **green olives** (stoned first) added in the last few minutes give interesting pungency to most meats and some fish.

It's easy to overdo **Worcestershire sauce**, but in small doses it is tasty and useful in stews and solid soups. Interesting to note that anchovies are a main ingredient. **Soy sauce** is essential for Chinese cooking, and for heightening flavour in all sorts of soups, casseroles, etc. **Sesame** in its various forms – seeds, paste (tahini) and oil – is a boon in winter soups and stews as well as in Chinese and Middle Eastern dishes. The seeds can be roasted or fried with vegetables. There are two kinds of oil, one pale and the other darker, tastier and more expensive: it's worth trying to track it down.

Which bring us to the whole question of which **oils**, when and where. I like to have one or two special ones for a splash of luxury where their taste really counts (persuade people to give you bottles of them instead of perfume at Christmas), in addition to the cheaper neutral-flavoured ones for frying and everyday salads where distinctive taste is contributed by other ingredients. **Sunflower** and **safflower** are more expensive than "mixed vegetable" but are polyunsaturated and so not geared to furring your arteries.

With more highly flavoured (and highly priced) types, choose the one that will enhance a specific dish. **Walnut**, for instance, has a pronounced nutty flavour that is superb in leafy salads; it is nutritious, but relatively expensive and does not keep indefinitely. The dark **sesame oil** is wonderful in Chinese food: add a spoonful before serving so that the flavour is right up front.

"Extra Virgin" **olive oil** is produced from the first cold pressing of the olives, and is thus most pungent and precious. Green and viscous, it's like some benevolent and fragrant lubricant for all the more inaccessible human parts. The paler cheaper version, called merely "pure" olive oil, is hardly worth buying: where extra virgin olive oil is *too* thick and strong-tasting for your salad dressing, mayonnaise or basil/garlic pasta anointing, dilute it a little with some lighter vegetable oil.

BASIC BULK

I keep the "dry goods" shelves of my store cupboard well stocked with all sorts of cereals, dried beans and peas and grains as well as variations on the flour theme. These I buy from wholefood stores whose rapid turnover ensures that chick peas will not remain bullets after five hours' boiling, and lentils are not rubbing shoulders with grit.

Pasta is *the* cheap-and-cheerful food. Italian designers spend years thinking up chic new shapes, gauging the subtly different sauce-retention capacities of a tube or a twist or a shell. The long noodles – spaghetti and tagliatelle – are best for relatively dry sauces. Keep packets of dry pasta of different shapes in the cupboard, and some fresh pasta (which needs only 3 or 4 minutes' cooking) in the freezer.

The most convenient all-purpose **rice** is the long-grain easy-cook sort, which produces dry separate grains. Good to accompany savoury dishes, and foolproof in risottos. Avoid brand-names – they are more expensive. Basmati is dearer, too, but its flavour is worthwhile with Indian or Middle Eastern recipes. Brown rice is more wholesome than white, but takes at least twice as long to cook. It can be used instead of white in most dishes – bearing in mind it has a nuttier flavour. As alternatives to rice in risotto-type dishes I sometimes cook **millet**, **cracked wheat** (bulgar or burghul), **roasted buckwheat** (kasha), or **couscous** (made from semolina) – all of which are delicious cold in salads, too.

I keep appropriate refined and wholewheat **flours** for pastry, cakes and bread. To ring the changes I use buckwheat flour (don't be put off by its grey speckled colour: it's rich in potassium and especially useful in gluten-free diets) for blinis, pancakes and Breton crêpes; its strong taste can be toned down by mixing with an equal measure of wheat flour. Polenta, the coarse meal ground from maize or Indian corn and beloved of Italians, has a bland comforting taste and is a good flavour-absorber. Finer cornmeal I use occasionally, for tortillas and cornbread. Highly refined cornflour/cornstarch is useful for thickening sauces.

CANS AND THE FREEZER

The only canned foods I make a point of stocking are **tomatoes** (often cheaper and better-flavoured than fresh ones: salt is usually the only added ingredient); **chick peas** (for emergencies when there's not time to cook dried ones); some **fish** (tuna, sardines and anchovies); and the odd can of consommé, which can stand in for home-made stock at a pinch if one disguises the strong taste of tin. Or is it monosodium glutamate? MSG is my single culinary phobia, bearable only in Japanese smoked oysters and seaweed crackers. Discovering how much fresher and rewarding home-cooked Chinese dishes are without this deadly leveller was one of my great cooking revelations.

In my recently acquired freezer I keep **bread**, a variety of **meats**, no **fish** (I find frozen fish watery), some **vegetables** (such as petits pois), and always a roll or two of commercial **puff pastry**, invaluable as a swanky container for homely mixtures such as smoked fish pie that may call for dressing up. It thaws in an hour and turns leftover scraps into glamorous ''puffs'' in no time at all.

SEND IN THE SUBSTITUTES

Part of the skill of creative improvising lies in substituting like with almost-like: using honey where you might have used sugar, or shallots for onions. Seek out alternatives in wholefood stores: **carob powder** has no caffeine, less fat and tastes sweeter than cocoa; **soft tofu** can be used instead of cream cheese in pâtés and mousses, instead of eggs in quiches and flans. **Firm tofu**, cut in squares like solid cheese, adds healthier protein to meatless stir-fry dishes. Learning this game of substitutes is not only good practice for when you run out of something; it can mean economies and/or healthier eating and, better still, it opens the way to new culinary discoveries of your own.

A NOTE ON QUANTITIES

SERVINGS

All the recipes make 6 reasonably sized servings unless otherwise indicated.

MEASURING INGREDIENTS

Quantities in the recipes are given in metric and imperial measures in the left-hand column, and in American weight and volume measures in the right. The equivalents given are approximate conversions, sometimes rounded up or down slightly to make measuring convenient: follow one system or another throughout a recipe.

OVEN TEMPERATURES

North American cooks should follow the Fahrenheit (°F) setting in the middle column throughout the book

	°C	°F	Gas Mark	
Very cool	110	225	¼	meringues
	120	250	½	
Cool	140	275	1	rich cakes
	150	300	2	baked custards; rice puddings
Moderate	160	325	3	cakes
	180	350	4	casseroles, stews
Moderately hot	190	375	5	casseroles
Fairly hot	200	400	6	roast meat; short pastry
Hot	220	425	7	puff pastry
	230	450	8	Yorkshire pudding
Very hot	240	475	9	

BACK TO BASICS

One of the problems with books written by experts is that by the time
they have acquired the experience and practice that expertise implies,
they tend to have forgotten just how little they knew when they started.
Experience inevitably teaches one confidence, and confidence is probably
the most useful tool in a cook's *batterie de cuisine.* So how does one
short-cut the process, acquiring confidence before one has cooked one's
way, via thousands of meals, to experience? One way, I believe, is
deliberately to think small. Instead of picking out recipes at random, fix
upon one limited area, like cooking rice, and work through it till it holds
no terrors or surprises any more. By the time your investigation is
complete you will have absorbed much useful information almost without
realizing it. And besides this you will have learned, and it is a valuable
lesson, that confident simplicity equals true sophistication.

SHORTCRUST PASTRY

Pastry is a fetish to some people — how light, how soft, how melting can it be? This is fine for perfectionists, but actually pastry can be stiff or hard or crumbly or elastic, or any number of other qualities, and still be right. It all depends what you want. So don't worry — almost any way you put together flour, fat and a little water will turn into pastry. This recipe is for a basic useful all-purpose pastry.

MAKES 225 g/8 oz/1⅔ cup QUANTITY

METRIC/IMPERIAL
225 g/8 oz plain or self-raising flour
pinch of salt
150 g/5 oz cold butter
squeeze of lemon juice
3—4 tbsp cold water

AMERICAN
1⅔ cups all-purpose or self-rising flour
pinch of salt
10 tbsp cold butter
squeeze of lemon juice
3—4 tbsp cold water

Put the flour and salt in a bowl and cut in the butter with a knife in each hand. Then break up the butter in the flour with your fingertips, so that it becomes crumby. Sprinkle the lemon juice and water over, stirring with a knife. Finally, gather it together into a ball, adding more water, if needed. Knead it briefly to make a dough without cracks. Put in a cool place to rest for about 20 minutes, long enough to preheat the oven. Roll out the pastry on a floured surface.

RICH SHORTCRUST PASTRY
This is made in exactly the same way, using 175 g/6 oz/1½ sticks of butter and adding 1 egg yolk. Because of the egg yolk, you will need only a little over 1 tablespoon of water to make a dough.

CHEESE PASTRY
Add 75 g/3 oz/¾ cup finely grated Cheddar or Parmesan cheese to the Rich Shortcrust Pastry.

SWEET PASTRY
Add 1 tablespoon icing/confectioners sugar to the Rich Shortcrust Pastry.

ROUGH PUFF PASTRY

Rough puff pastry is not at all difficult to make, and it's most exciting to see a well-risen pie. It may not be quite as flaky and risen as puff pastry, but it is far less laborious and will taste better when cold.

To ensure success, have everything, including your hands, as cold as possible. The best time and place to make rough puff pastry is in a really dreary cold kitchen in winter. (The week of January 12, 1986, was a vintage pastry week!) Handle the pastry as little as possible: mix with a knife.

This quantity of pastry will line and cover a 20–23 cm/ 8–9 inch round sandwich/layer cake tin, or cover a 23 × 30 cm/ 9 × 12 inch deep pie dish.

METRIC/IMPERIAL
225 g/8 oz flour
pinch of salt
175 g/6 oz cold butter or
   hard margarine
about 150 ml/¼ pint iced
   water
squeeze of lemon juice

AMERICAN
1⅔ cups flour
pinch of salt
1½ sticks cold butter or
   hard margarine
about ⅔ cup iced water
squeeze of lemon juice

Put the flour and salt in a mixing bowl. Chop up the hard fat, straight from the refrigerator, into about 40 squares. Stir it into the flour with a knife, sprinkle on the iced water and lemon juice, stir around, and then very quickly form into a rough ball shape with your hands.

Put on to a lightly floured surface, and roll it out into a rectangle about 15 × 30 cm/6 × 12 inches. (It won't be an even shape yet, but don't worry.) Fold the bottom third towards the centre, and bring the top third down on it. Turn the pastry round so the folds are to the side. Press the edges together, and roll out as before. Fold again, and turn. Press the edges together, roll and fold once more. Put the pastry to get very cold again in the refrigerator for at least half an hour.

The point of the rolling and folding is to spread the fat evenly but to keep it in layers, and also to trap air in between the layers of pastry. When you put the pastry in a hot oven, the air expands and blows the pastry up. That's why it's important to press the edges together, so that you don't roll all the air out from between the layers.

Take the pastry out of the refrigerator, and roll and fold at least another two or three times. You can now use it right away, or keep it in a cold place and use next day, or freeze. It's a good idea to make more than you need, and freeze the rest.

Bake in a hot oven (230°C/450°F/Gas Mark 8).

SUET PASTRY

This quantity is sufficient for a 900 ml–1.2 litre/1½–2 pint pudding basin/1 quart steaming mould.

MAKES 225 g/8 oz/1⅔ cup QUANTITY

METRIC/IMPERIAL
225 g/8 oz self-raising flour,
   or plain flour and 2 tsp
   baking powder
pinch of salt
50 g/2 oz fresh
   breadcrumbs (optional)
115 g/4 oz shredded suet
about 120 ml/4 fl oz water

Mix the flour, baking powder, if used, and salt. Add the breadcrumbs, if used (they give a lighter dough), and suet, and mix. Sprinkle on the water and stir with a knife, then form into a soft dough with your hands. You may need a little more water.

Roll out lightly on a floured surface. Suet pastry is usually used about 1–2.5 cm/½–1 inch thick.

Use for steamed puddings with fruit, meat or vegetable fillings (make them in layers for hearty appetites). Or for dumplings, take the dough before rolling out, form into egg-size balls and drop into boiling soup or hot stew. Cook these for about 15 minutes, covered with a lid.

AMERICAN
1⅔ cups self-rising flour, or
   all-purpose flour and 2
   tsp baking powder
pinch of salt
1 cup fresh bread crumbs
   (optional)
1 scant cup shredded suet
about ½ cup water

BASIC CRÊPE BATTER

METRIC/IMPERIAL
115 g/4 oz flour
pinch of salt
2 eggs
300 ml/½ pint milk or mixed
  milk and water
1 tbsp melted butter or oil

AMERICAN
¾ cup flour
pinch of salt
2 eggs
1¼ cups milk or mixed milk
  and water
1 tbsp melted butter or oil

Put the flour and salt in a mixing bowl. Make a well, and put in the eggs and a little milk. Beat, adding the rest of the milk. (Or put all ingredients into a blender.) If possible, let the batter stand for 1–2 hours. This will allow the starch grains to swell, and it will make a softer crêpe. Add the butter or oil just before using. The batter will keep for a day or so.

This batter is also suitable for Yorkshire puddings and toad-in-the-hole.

FOR YORKSHIRE PUDDING

Melt 1 tablespoon dripping (or use the fat from a roast) in a 20 × 30 cm/8 × 12 inch baking tin in a hot oven (220°C/425°F/Gas Mark 7). Pour in the batter when the fat is really hot and bake for at least 30 minutes.

BASIC WHITE SAUCE

MAKES 300 ml/½ pint/1¼ cups

METRIC/IMPERIAL
25 g/1 oz butter
25 g/1 oz flour
300 ml/½ pint milk

AMERICAN
2 tbsp butter
3 tbsp flour
1¼ cups milk

Melt the butter in a small saucepan over a moderate heat. Add the flour and stir in until absorbed. This mixture is called a roux. Add a little milk to the pan and let it get warm, before stirring it into the roux. Gradually add the remaining milk, allowing it to warm in the pan each time before incorporating it, to prevent any lumps forming.

This is a base which can now be made into either a sweet or savoury sauce.

For a thick sauce, to bind meat or fish into croquettes, use 150 ml/¼ pint/⅔ cup milk.

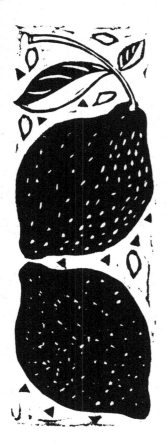

 For a thinner sauce, use 450 ml/¾ pint/2 cups milk or milk and water.

 To make a richer sauce, add a little cream, or stir in a beaten egg and reheat, but don't boil.

 Mustard, curry powder, anchovy essence or capers, can all be added to the basic roux.

VARIATIONS
BÉCHAMEL SAUCE
Simmer a slice of onion, a blade of mace, and a bay leaf in the milk for 5 minutes, then strain and add to the roux. Season with salt and pepper.

PARSLEY SAUCE
Add 2 tablespoons chopped fresh parsley to the white sauce, with salt and pepper to taste.

CHEESE SAUCE
Stir 50 g/2 oz/½ cup grated cheese, either strong Cheddar or Parmesan, into the hot sauce.

BASIC BROWN SAUCE

MAKES 300 ml/½ pint/1¼ cups

METRIC/IMPERIAL
25 g/1 oz butter or dripping
25 g/1 oz flour
300 ml/½ pint stock
salt and pepper

Melt the fat, add the flour, and cook until the flour turns brown. (This is a brown roux.) Now add the stock gradually, stirring it well as the sauce cooks.

This is a base for all kinds of variations, to be served mostly with meat.

AMERICAN
2 tbsp butter or drippings
3 tbsp flour
1¼ cups stock
salt and pepper

 Add redcurrant jelly, capers, chopped orange, sherry or Marsala.

 Cook a little chopped onion in the fat and add a few chopped gherkins.

ONION SAUCE

This is one of the most versatile English sauces. It comes in particularly handy for heating up leftover lamb or chicken. Slices of cold meat covered with onion sauce and gently heated, served with baked potatoes and redcurrant jelly, are a treat reminiscent of childhood.

METRIC/IMPERIAL
225 g/8 oz onions, peeled and finely chopped
25 g/1 oz butter or margarine
25 g/1 oz flour
about 300 ml/½ pint milk
ground mace or grated nutmeg
salt and black pepper

Put the onions in a small saucepan with just enough water to cover. Stew gently till the onions are soft and translucent. Most of the water will have disappeared, but strain off any that's left and keep it to add to the sauce.

Make a white sauce by melting the butter, adding the flour and cooking a little, then adding the onion juice. Stir, and add enough milk to make a thick sauce. Add a shake of mace or nutmeg and salt and pepper to taste. Stir in the onions. (You will find that this will make the sauce thinner, so be sure to have it rather solid before.)

AMERICAN
½ lb onions, peeled and finely chopped
2 tbsp butter or margarine
3 tbsp flour
about 1¼ cups milk
ground mace or grated nutmeg
salt and black pepper

TOMATO SPAGHETTI SAUCE

The pork adds an extra dimension to the taste of this sauce, but if you want a vegetarian sauce, then of course it must be omitted. It is interesting to try various different herbs — bay leaf and basil is one version, but oregano or marjoram are also very good. It is feasible to add more tomato paste, which will make an exceedingly strong sauce. Italians would use a much larger quantity of oil than is advised here.
Serve with 450 g/1 lb of pasta as a main dish for 4 people.

METRIC/IMPERIAL
2 tbsp olive oil
3 cloves garlic, peeled and chopped
2 tbsp chopped onion
150-g/5-oz can tomato paste
1 slice pork belly or unsmoked bacon, minced or very finely chopped
2 × 400-g/14-oz cans Italian plum tomatoes, chopped
1 tbsp chopped fresh parsley
1 tbsp chopped fresh basil, or 1 tsp dried basil
1 bay leaf
½ tsp sugar
salt and black pepper

Put the olive oil in a heavy saucepan and heat, then add the garlic and onion and cook until lightly browned. Add the tomato paste and cook briefly, stirring so that it doesn't stick. Now add all the other ingredients, including the juice from the tomatoes, plus about half a tomato can of water. Bring to the boil and simmer gently for at least 30 minutes, or up to 1 hour.

AMERICAN
2 tbsp olive oil
3 cloves garlic, peeled and chopped
2 tbsp chopped onion
5-oz can tomato paste
1 slice fresh pork side (belly) or bacon, ground or very finely chopped
2 × 14-oz cans Italian plum tomatoes, chopped
1 tbsp chopped fresh parsley
1 tbsp chopped fresh basil, or 1 tsp dried basil
1 bay leaf
½ tsp sugar
salt and black pepper

BOLOGNESE SAUCE

In Italy, a Bolognese sauce is referred to as a *ragù*, which shows it's much more of a meat and vegetable mini-stew than just a plain meat or tomato sauce. Exact proportions vary like anything, especially in the amount of tomato purée to use; this recipe has more than some, as we seem to have got used to a tomatoey version. Wine definitely improves the flavour, but if you haven't any, use a little red wine vinegar and grape juice. People who are used to spaghetti or macaroni with a meat or tomato sauce will tend to say with surprise "How is it your sauce tastes so good?", not realizing all the subtlety of it, and how many ingredients have gone into it. Long slow cooking is the secret, too.

Serve it with almost any kind of pasta, except the very fine ones, like vermicelli.

METRIC/IMPERIAL
butter and olive oil for frying
115 g/4 oz unsmoked bacon (thick cut), chopped
2 carrots, peeled and chopped
1 stick celery, chopped
1 large onion, peeled and chopped
225 g/8 oz minced beef
115 g/4 oz chicken livers, chopped
225 ml/8 fl oz beef stock
3 tbsp tomato purée
120 ml/4 fl oz red wine
1 bay leaf
freshly grated nutmeg
salt and black pepper
a little cream

This sauce should simmer gently for at least 30 minutes, so get it going on the stove before you cook the pasta.

In a heavy pot or pan, heat a little butter and olive oil. Brown the bacon and vegetables, stirring them well so they don't stick, then add the beef and chicken livers and cook until the beef turns brown.

Add the stock, tomato purée and wine and stir well. Put in the bay leaf, and grate in a little nutmeg. Add salt and black pepper to taste. Bring to the boil, cover tightly, turn down the heat, and let the sauce simmer for at least 30 minutes. It will be fine just ticking over on the stove for up to an hour. Or you can make it in advance, and reheat just before you cook the pasta.

Before serving, check the seasoning, and add a couple of tablespoons of cream.

AMERICAN
butter and olive oil for frying
¼ lb slab bacon, chopped
2 carrots, peeled and chopped
1 stalk celery, chopped
1 large onion, peeled and chopped
½ lb ground beef
¼ lb chicken livers, chopped
1 cup beef stock
3 tbsp tomato paste
½ cup red wine
1 bay leaf
freshly grated nutmeg
salt and black pepper
a little cream

THICK MAYONNAISE

A mayonnaise made in small quantities, but very solid, this can be kept in a lidded jar in the refrigerator for at least one month. The recipe sounds very rich — but if you use it as a base, adding spoonfuls of yogurt, or more lemon juice, or a little milk or thin cream and horseradish, for instance, you can make a whole gamut of interesting instant sauces. To make aïoli, add garlic and some more olive oil and lemon juice as required. All these go very well indeed with plain vegetables, adding a delicious richness.

METRIC/IMPERIAL
3 fresh egg yolks
½ tsp Dijon mustard
juice of ½ lemon
salt and black or white
   pepper
300 ml/½ pint olive oil

Put the egg yolks into a bowl with a wide base. Mix in the mustard, and a generous squeeze of lemon. This stops the oil from separating later. Season with a pinch of salt and a few grinds of pepper. Gradually add the oil in a tiny trickle at first down the side of the bowl, mixing it in all the time with a wooden spoon. Don't try pouring the oil out of a large bottle — the bigger the bottle, the more comes out! So transfer the required quantity into a small jug for pouring.

After a while the mixture will get a smooth glassy look to it: now you add the oil continuously in quite a generous stream. If the mayonnaise gets very solid, add some more lemon juice. It won't take very long, and I have never known it to curdle. If the oil does separate, and the mixture is not one smooth surface, but blotchy, try adding a little hot water, or start with another egg yolk in another bowl, and add the separated mixture to it gradually. It won't matter having one more egg yolk — I have known people to use 4 egg yolks to begin with.

AMERICAN
3 fresh egg yolks
½ tsp Dijon-style mustard
juice of ½ lemon
salt and black or white
   pepper
1¼ cups olive oil

VINAIGRETTE DRESSING

Combine virgin olive oil and red or white wine vinegar in the proportion of 4 parts oil to 1 part vinegar. Flavour with crushed garlic, a little mustard and salt and black pepper to taste. This can be varied by using half sunflower oil and half walnut oil, flavoured with chopped walnuts instead of the mustard. Or use cider vinegar, or one of the fruit-flavoured vinegars – raspberry, blackcurrant or sour cherry.

TZATZIKI

This is the Greek name for a thick sauce made with cucumber and yogurt, which can either be served on its own, with bread, as a first course, or put on the table to be spooned into vegetable soups. Or it can be used as a dip, or a sauce with fish, or, especially good, with vegetable fritters.

METRIC/IMPERIAL
1 small cucumber
225 ml/8 fl oz Greek-style strained yogurt
2 cloves garlic, peeled and crushed
fresh mint leaves, finely chopped
salt and black pepper

AMERICAN
1 cucumber
1 cup thick plain yogurt
2 cloves garlic, peeled and minced
fresh mint leaves, finely chopped
salt and black pepper

Grate the cucumber, without peeling it, into a bowl and leave for a few minutes so that the juices will run out a little. Pour these off, or squeeze out. Mix into the yogurt gradually, so that you can reserve some cucumber if you want a creamier, thinner sauce. Add the garlic and mint. (If you haven't got any mint, it tastes very good without.) Add salt and pepper if needed, but with yogurt sauces it is not always necessary.

If you are wary of guests not liking garlic, only use one clove. If you omit the garlic altogether, increase the amount of mint.

SAUCE RÉMOULADE

A very useful sharp sauce, for chops, fish or vegetables. Use home-made mayonnaise (see page 27) or a good bought one. For a lighter, more economical mixture, use a lesser quantity of mayonnaise and add a stiffly whisked egg white, or a little plain yogurt.

METRIC/IMPERIAL
300 ml/½ pint mayonnaise
2 tsp Dijon mustard
1 tsp chopped capers
1 tsp chopped gherkins
1 tsp chopped mixed herbs
1 tsp anchovy essence, or 2
  anchovy fillets, finely
  chopped

Mix all the ingredients together.

 This mixing of a fishy taste into a sauce to be used for meat goes way back to Roman times — to a sauce called *liquamen*.

AMERICAN
1¼ cups mayonnaise
2 tsp Dijon-style mustard
1 tsp chopped capers
1 tsp chopped gherkins
1 tsp chopped mixed herbs
½ tsp anchovy paste, or 2
  anchovy fillets, finely
  chopped

PESTO

This sauce should be thick and pungent. Use it on pasta, in soups, on baked potatoes, or spread on bread. Make it in a larger quantity whenever you are lucky enough to find a good source of fresh basil, and store in a tight-fitting jar.

METRIC/IMPERIAL
50 g/2 oz fresh basil, or 15 g/
  ½ oz dried basil
2 cloves, garlic, peeled
50 g/2 oz pine nuts
salt and black pepper
50 g/2 oz Parmesan cheese,
  freshly grated
100 ml/3½ fl oz olive oil

Blend all the ingredients together in a blender or food processor. If making by hand, in a mortar, pound the basil, garlic, pine nuts and salt and pepper to a paste, then stir in the cheese and gradually stir in the oil.

AMERICAN
2 oz fresh basil (about 1 cup
  loosely packed) or ½ cup
  dried basil
2 cloves garlic, peeled
⅔ cup pine nuts
salt and black pepper
½ cup freshly grated
  Parmesan cheese
7 tbsp olive oil

WALNUT SAUCE

A blender is best for making this sauce.

METRIC/IMPERIAL
50 g/2 oz shelled walnuts,
    chopped
50 g/2 oz fresh parsley,
    chopped
2 tbsp fresh breadcrumbs
25 g/1 oz butter
120 ml/4 fl oz olive oil
2 tbsp milk
salt and black pepper

Blend together the walnuts, parsley, breadcrumbs, butter and oil. Stir in the milk, and season to taste with salt and pepper. Serve with pasta or fish.

AMERICAN
½ cup chopped walnuts
1 cup chopped parsley
2 tbsp fresh bread crumbs
2 tbsp butter
½ cup olive oil
2 tbsp milk
salt and black pepper

MAKING BREADCRUMBS

FRESH BREADCRUMBS
Used for gratin dishes, in suet pastry, for stuffings, etc. Crumble a stale wholemeal or white loaf in the fingers, or grate, or use a food processor. Store the crumbs in a plastic bag in the refrigerator or freezer.

TOASTED BREADCRUMBS
Used to coat rissoles, etc. Can also be used as a topping. Put slices of stale bread into a slow oven (140°C/275°F/Gas Mark 1) to bake till dry and golden brown. Crush with a rolling-pin, spreading the crumbs out well so that all are finely crushed. For very fine crumbs, put through a sieve. Store in a covered jar. They will keep for a long time.

CROUTONS FOR SOUP
Cut bread in thick slices and then dice. Fry in oil or oil and butter until golden brown. Add garlic, herbs or curry powder to the fat, to make savoury croutons.

FAST FOOD

Commercial fast food may lack finesse and charm, but there is no reason to equate speedy preparation with second best in food. The recipes in this chapter have only this in common, that they detain you for the least possible time over a hot stove. Indeed, some need no cooking at all. People who are forever cooking against the clock will find a hundred uses for a food processor; a pressure cooker brings slow cooking items like chick peas into the fast food category; a steamer allows vegetables to be left to take care of themselves while you get on with the serious preparation. But, on reflection, the fast cook's — indeed, any cook's — most valuable piece of equipment is a set of razor-sharp knives. Also buy a knife sharpener and teach yourself how to use it — not just now and then but as a regular ritual.

SASHIMI

With gravad lax and seviche on every trendy menu, raw fish no longer seems outlandish. For a sophisticated occasion, sashimi — thin slices of the finest, freshest fish available, served with a hot horseradish paste and soy sauce — makes a delicate treat worth chatting up your fishmonger for. I have been served sashimi consisting of three impeccable cubes of salmon, tuna and bass, the colours in pretty contrast: peach, rose-red and milky white. Any firm fish can be used, but so little is needed that it may be worth going for the best. Green wasabi powder, hotter but more subtle than horseradish as we know it, can be found in oriental grocers. Presentation of sashimi is important. Plain white or black plates are flattering, failing authentic Japanese pottery, with sauce in tiny individual bowls.

METRIC/IMPERIAL

100 g/4 oz each of any three of the following fish: salmon, sole, sea bass, tuna, red snapper or bream, filleted and skinned (prepared weight)

a selection of vegetables such as carrots, cucumber, celery and mooli

4 tbsp shoyu or Japanese soy sauce

1 tsp grated fresh ginger

1 tbsp wasabi, mixed to a paste with a little water

AMERICAN

¼ lb each of any three of the following fish: salmon, sole, bass, tuna, red snapper or porgy, filleted and skinned (prepared weight)

a selection of vegetables such as carrots, cucumber, celery and daikon

4 tbsp shoyu or Japanese soy sauce

1 tsp grated fresh ginger root

1 tbsp wasabi, mixed to a paste with a little water

Keep the fish refrigerated till just before serving. Peel and slice the vegetables into fine strips, and crisp in iced water. Mix the shoyu and ginger, and divide between bowls. Put a little mound of wasabi paste on each serving plate.

With a very sharp knife, cut the fish into thin slices diagonally, except for tuna, which is cut straight across. Arrange the fish on the plates with the vegetables in thin clusters. Guests eat fish alternately with vegetables, for contrasting taste and texture, dipping in one or both sauces.

PAPAYA AND AVOCADO
WITH GINGER AND LEMON
DRESSING

The point about this combination is that it looks beautiful, and only takes a minute to prepare. Also, if your fruit are ripe but firm, and your hand is steady when slicing, it can stretch one avocado and one papaya four ways. Failing preserved ginger, substitute a little runny chutney juice to which you add a squeeze of lemon, and maybe a pinch of grated fresh ginger. Because avocado blackens when exposed to the air, it must be prepared at the last minute.

METRIC/IMPERIAL
1 large or 2 small papayas
1 large or 2 small avocados
2 tbsp liquid from preserved
 ginger
juice of ½ lemon

Peel and halve the papaya and scoop out the seeds. With a sharp knife, peel the avocado, cut around lengthways and remove the stone. Cut each fruit half in two, then slice thinly lengthways. Arrange green and pink slices in fans on each plate.

For the dressing, stir together the ginger liquid and lemon juice. Spoon in a disc to one side of the fruit slices on each plate. If for any reason the salad has to wait, sprinkle more lemon juice over the avocado slices to stop them discolouring.

AMERICAN
1 large or 2 small papayas
1 large or 2 small avocados
2 tbsp liquid from preserved
 ginger
juice of ½ lemon

CRAB SOUP

METRIC/IMPERIAL
225 g/8 oz crabmeat, fresh, frozen or canned
1 onion, peeled and finely chopped
25 g/1 oz butter
600 ml/1 pint chicken or fish stock, or water and a stock cube
1 tbsp tomato purée
1 small glass sherry
salt and black pepper
a little cream or plain yogurt
cayenne pepper or paprika

Soften the onion in the butter. Stir in the crab, then add the stock and tomato purée. Bring to the boil, and simmer for 5 minutes. Remove from the heat and stir in the sherry. Test for seasoning.

Serve topped with a spoonful of cream or yogurt in each soup bowl and sprinkled with cayenne or paprika.

✎ Canned mackerel fillets can be used instead of crab, or prawns/shrimp.

AMERICAN
½ lb crabmeat, fresh, frozen or canned
1 onion, peeled and finely chopped
2 tbsp butter
2½ cups chicken or fish stock, or water and a bouillon cube
1 tbsp tomato paste
1 small glass sherry
salt and black pepper
a little cream or plain yogurt
cayenne or paprika

CORN CHOWDER

SERVES 4–6

METRIC/IMPERIAL
175 g/6 oz sweetcorn kernels, drained if canned
1 medium onion, peeled and finely chopped
25 g/1 oz butter
225 g/8 oz potatoes, peeled and sliced
900 ml/1½ pints milk
1 chicken stock cube, crumbled
200-g/7-oz can mackerel with its juices
1 tsp dried tarragon
2.5 cm/1 in cube fresh ginger, peeled and grated
black pepper

Soften the onion in the butter in a saucepan. Add the potatoes, and cook for a few minutes on moderate heat. Add all the rest of the ingredients, and simmer for at least 30 minutes.

Check seasoning before serving. (It should not need any salt, because of the stock cube.)

AMERICAN
1 cup corn kernels, drained if canned
1 medium onion, peeled and finely chopped
2 tbsp butter
½ lb potatoes, peeled and sliced
3¾ cups milk
1 chicken bouillon cube, crumbled
7-oz can mackerel with its juices
1 tsp dried tarragon
1 in cube fresh ginger root, peeled and grated
black pepper

WINTER PEA SOUP

METRIC/IMPERIAL
225 g/8 oz split green peas
2 onions, peeled and sliced
100 g/4 oz potato, peeled and diced
2.5 cm/1 in cube fresh ginger, peeled
2 tbsp ground cumin
1 tbsp ground coriander
1.5 litres/2½ pints chicken stock or water
1–2 tbsp lemon juice
salt

Put all the ingredients, except the lemon juice and salt, into a saucepan and bring to the boil. Cover and simmer until cooked – about 30 minutes. (Don't put any salt in at the beginning.)

When everything is soft and tender, fish out the ginger cube. Add the lemon juice and salt to taste. Either blend until smooth in a blender or food processor or use a potato masher or fork if you prefer a rougher texture. Reheat and taste for seasoning. The soup is now ready to serve.

AMERICAN
1 heaping cup split green peas
2 onions, peeled and sliced
⅔ cup peeled and diced potato
1 in cube fresh ginger root, peeled
2 tbsp ground cumin
1 tbsp ground coriander
1½ quarts chicken stock or water
1–2 tbsp lemon juice
salt

MUSHROOM SOUP

This soup really does need a good stock — one made from the remains of a roast chicken, for instance.

METRIC/IMPERIAL
225 g/8 oz button mushrooms, finely chopped
1 onion, peeled and finely chopped
2 cloves garlic, peeled and finely chopped
75 g/3 oz butter
1 tbsp flour
1.2 litres/2 pints chicken stock
2 tbsp cream
1 tbsp chopped parsley
salt and black pepper
1 tbsp oil
4 slices bread, cut into cubes

Soften the onion and one garlic clove in 25 g/1 oz/ 2 tbsp of butter. Add the mushrooms, and let them cook gently for a few minutes. Add the flour and stir in well. Pour on the stock, stirring. Bring to the boil, then cover the saucepan and let the soup simmer for about 20 minutes. Add the cream, parsley and salt and pepper to taste.

Heat the rest of the butter with the oil and the remaining garlic in a frying pan. Fry the bread cubes till brown.

Pour the soup into hot bowls, and scatter the fried bread cubes over. You can also add grated Parmesan or Cheddar cheese, or serve it separately.

AMERICAN
½ lb button mushrooms, finely chopped
1 onion, peeled and finely chopped
2 cloves garlic, peeled and finely chopped
6 tbsp butter
1 tbsp flour
5 cups chicken stock
2 tbsp cream
1 tbsp chopped parsley
salt and black pepper
1 tbsp oil
4 slices bread, cut into cubes

GENOESE PAN PIZZA

Although pizzas are usually made with a yeast dough, Genoese pizzas are often made with a simpler base.

METRIC/IMPERIAL
225 g/8 oz self-raising flour
1 tsp salt
1 tsp mixed dried herbs
about 6 tbsp water
oil for frying

TOPPING
2 tbsp tomato purée
4 tomatoes, sliced
200-g/7-oz can tuna,
    drained and oil reserved
2 tsp capers
about 12 black olives,
    stoned and chopped
100 g/4 oz Cheddar cheese,
    grated

Mix the flour, salt, herbs and water together to make a soft dough, adding about 2 tablespoons of the oil from the can of tuna. Divide the dough into four, and roll each piece out to a round about 12.5 cm/5 in diameter.

Put a little oil in a frying pan and cook one dough round for about 2 minutes on each side, till it turns colour. Remove, and brown the remaining rounds.

Cover each round with tomato purée then sliced tomato, then tuna, capers and chopped olives. Top with grated cheese and grill/broil until bubbling and hot.

AMERICAN
1⅔ cups self-rising flour
1 tsp salt
1 tsp mixed dried herbs
about 6 tbsp water
oil for frying

TOPPING
2 tbsp tomato paste
4 tomatoes, sliced
7-oz can tuna, drained and
    oil reserved
2 tsp capers
about 12 black olives, pitted
    and chopped
1 cup grated Cheddar
    cheese

SUMMERY SOUP

METRIC/IMPERIAL
300 ml/½ pint plain low-fat
    yogurt
300 ml/½ pint tomato juice
juice of 1 orange
squeeze of lemon juice
a few fresh mint leaves,
    chopped
a little chopped parsley
salt and black pepper

Mix all the ingredients well together, by hand or in a blender or food processor. Decorate with a little extra parsley or a sprig of mint. Chill and serve cold.

AMERICAN
1¼ cups plain low-fat
    yogurt
1¼ cups tomato juice
juice of 1 orange
squeeze of lemon juice
a few fresh mint leaves,
    chopped
a little chopped parsley
salt and black pepper

RAMEKINS OF SMOKED HADDOCK WITH TOMATO AND CREAM

An example of what I think of as innocent food, simple but pleasing when the ingredients are right — in this case the tomatoes must be fresh, and ripe. Canned tomatoes, though invaluable, taste acrid in this sort of melange. Leftover haddock can be used though, and crème fraîche or soured cream add a refreshing sharpness.

METRIC/IMPERIAL
1 small smoked haddock
   fillet
4 large or 6–8 medium
   tomatoes, peeled, de-
   seeded and roughly
   chopped
salt and black pepper
120 ml/4 fl oz double cream
2 tbsp finely chopped fresh
   parsley

AMERICAN
1 small smoked haddock
   fillet (finnan haddie)
4 large or 6–8 medium
   tomatoes, peeled,
   deseeded and roughly
   chopped
salt and black pepper
½ cup heavy cream
2 tbsp finely chopped fresh
   parsley

Preheat the oven to moderate (180°C/350°F/Gas Mark 4).

Cook the haddock, skin side up, in a flat ovenproof dish with 2 or 3 tablespoons water, under a piece of foil, in the oven for about 10 minutes. Drain and leave to cool.

Distribute the tomatoes between ramekins. Remove skin and any bones from the haddock, flake gently and share out likewise. Add a tiny scatter of salt and lots of black pepper. Spoon the cream into each ramekin. Give them a little shake, then slide them on to a baking sheet. Cook for about 10 minutes in the oven, increased to fairly hot (200°C/400°F/Gas Mark 6).

Serve with a dusting of parsley, and chunks of brown bread to mop up the juices.

FRITTATA OF TOMATOES AND BASIL

A frittata is a solid kind of Italian omelette that you can slice and serve chunks off, and yet it is not remotely hard or leathery, but soft and creamy.
This looks like an alarming amount of oil, but don't worry — most of it is poured off. The cooking of the onions and tomatoes can be done in advance.

METRIC/IMPERIAL
400-g/14-oz can tomatoes, drained of liquid
675 g/1½ lb onions, peeled and finely sliced
5 tbsp olive oil
6 large eggs
2 tbsp grated cheese
2 tbsp chopped fresh basil
salt and black pepper
25 g/1 oz butter

AMERICAN
14-oz can tomatoes, drained of liquid
1½ lb onions, peeled and finely sliced
5 tbsp olive oil
6 large eggs
2 tbsp grated cheese
2 tbsp chopped fresh basil
salt and black pepper
2 tbsp butter

Cook the onions in the oil over a gentle heat until they are soft and golden. This will take some time; don't hurry them, let them just simmer gently. Now add the tomatoes, turn the heat up and cook for about 5 minutes, stirring, over a strong heat. Drain the oil off, and leave the onions and tomatoes to cool.

In a mixing bowl beat the eggs. Add the tomato and onion mixture, grated cheese, basil and salt and pepper to taste.

Make sure your guests are present and prepared to eat in 15 minutes. Heat a large frying pan, add the butter and pour in the egg mixture. Turn the heat right down to its lowest, and let the frittata cook very gently for about 15 minutes. There's no stirring to do; just let it heat through and set the eggs. After that, if the eggs are still unset in the middle, you can put it briefly under the grill/broiler to set the surface. But it should not be brown or hard, just gently set.

For *Frittata of asparagus* use 450 g/1 lb asparagus, 6 large eggs, 50 g/2 oz/½ cup freshly grated Parmesan cheese and 50 g/2 oz/4 tbsp butter. The asparagus can be canned or fresh. If canned, drain off liquid and cut into chunks. Cook fresh, trimmed asparagus until it is ''al dente'', then drain and cut into chunks before adding to the beaten eggs.

LINGUINE WITH TUNA AND ANCHOVIES

Linguine is the thin version of spaghetti. Vermicelli or thin Chinese noodles will do just as well.

METRIC/IMPERIAL
450 g/1 lb linguine
4 cloves garlic, peeled and finely chopped
100 ml/3½ fl oz olive oil
225 g/8 oz fresh tuna steak, or canned tuna, drained
black pepper
2 × 50-g/2-oz cans anchovy fillets, drained
50 g/2 oz black olives
freshly grated Parmesan cheese to serve

Warm a large ovenproof dish or serving dish in the oven.

Cook the linguine until just tender in well-salted boiling water. Meanwhile, brown the garlic in the olive oil. Grill/broil the fresh tuna; or, if using canned tuna, add it to the garlic oil and heat through.

Drain the cooked pasta and put in the hot dish. Pour over the garlic oil and fish. Grind a generous helping of black pepper on, and toss the pasta. Now arrange the anchovies, coiled around, and the black olives on top of the pasta. Leave for 5–10 minutes, then serve with grated cheese offered separately.

AMERICAN
1 lb linguine
4 cloves garlic, peeled and finely chopped
7 tbsp olive oil
½ lb fresh tuna steak, or canned tuna, drained
black pepper
2 × 2-oz cans anchovy fillets, drained
⅓ cup black olives
freshly grated Parmesan cheese to serve

PISSALADIÈRE

Use either the quick pan pizza dough in the recipe on page 38, or a similar quantity of bread dough, or simply bought muffins (English-style), split, as a base.

METRIC/IMPERIAL
450 g/1 lb onions, peeled and sliced
olive oil
1 clove
black pepper
50 g/2 oz black olives
50-g/2-oz can anchovy fillets, drained

Preheat the oven to hot (220°C/425°F/Gas Mark 7).

Cook the onions gently in olive oil, with the clove, until they are soft and mushy; discard the clove. Spread the onions thickly on the rolled-out dough or muffins. Pepper well. Dot with olives and anchovies. Bake for about 15 minutes.

AMERICAN
1 lb onions, peeled and sliced
olive oil
1 clove
black pepper
⅓ cup black olives
2-oz can anchovy fillets, drained

POTATO FRITTERS

Couldn't be more basic, or more delicious. These must be made and cooked in quick succession, or the potatoes will discolour.

SERVES 1

METRIC/IMPERIAL
1 medium potato, peeled
    and grated
a little grated onion
freshly grated nutmeg
salt and black pepper
oil and butter for frying

AMERICAN
1 medium potato, peeled
    and grated
a little grated onion
freshly grated nutmeg
salt and black pepper
oil and butter for frying

Mix together the potato and onion. Add a scrape of nutmeg and salt and pepper to taste. Press spoonfuls of the mixture in the palm of the hands, to squeeze out juice. Pat into flat round cakes, and fry in a mixture of oil and butter, turning several times. The fritters will go crisp and brown around the edges.

Serve with slices of corned beef and tomato relish or Tzatziki (page 28). Or with courgettes/zucchini cooked with dill.

CHEESE AND ONION SOUFFLÉ

There's no need to go through the business of making a white sauce as a base for a soufflé. I suppose you could really call this half soufflé, half omelette.

METRIC/IMPERIAL
175 g/6 oz mature Cheddar cheese, grated
675 g/1½ lb onions, peeled and finely chopped
50 g/2 oz butter
6 eggs, separated
1 tsp made mustard (French or Dijon)
salt and black pepper

Preheat the oven moderately hot (190C°/375°F/Gas Mark 5). Grease a soufflé dish or deep cake tin.

Gently cook the chopped onions in the butter until tender. Put into a mixing bowl. Add the beaten egg yolks, the grated cheese, mustard, a generous amount of black pepper and a little salt.

Check that the oven has reached the correct heat. Beat the egg whites till stiff, and fold into the onion mixture. Pour into the greased dish, and bake for about 20 minutes, or until the soufflé is risen. Serve at once.

AMERICAN
1½ cups grated sharp cheese
1½ lb onions, peeled and finely chopped
4 tbsp butter
6 eggs, separated
1 tsp Dijon-style mustard
salt and black pepper

ORECCHIETTE WITH BROCCOLI

Orecchiette means "little ears".

METRIC/IMPERIAL
350 g/12 oz orecchiette or pasta shells
450 g/1 lb broccoli
salt and black pepper
1 clove garlic, peeled and finely chopped
3 tbsp olive oil
50 g/2 oz Parmesan or Cheddar cheese, freshly grated

Trim any thick stalks off the broccoli, and chop the rest up. Put the pasta to cook in a large pan of boiling salted water. After 5 minutes, add the broccoli. Cook for another 10 minutes, or until the pasta and broccoli are both tender. Drain and return to the pan.

Fry the garlic in the olive oil. Put the pasta in a hot serving bowl, and pour the garlic oil over. Add the grated cheese, mix well and serve very hot.

AMERICAN
¾ lb orecchiette or pasta shells
1 lb broccoli
salt and black pepper
1 clove garlic, peeled and finely chopped
3 tbsp olive oil
½ cup freshly grated Parmesan or Cheddar cheese

CARPACCIO

Carpaccio, named after the Venetian painter, is thinly sliced
raw beef, served with a piquant sauce. As the meat is not
marinated, it is essential that it should be the tenderest cut,
otherwise it will be chewy and not very nice.
Try this dish out first — to see if you and your friends like
it — in a small amount, as an elegant first course, possibly on a
dish of mixed cooked meats, such as French and German
sausage, so that people have a choice. They may eat it and
enjoy it without knowing it's raw meat, if you don't tell them
till afterwards.
It's not easy to slice meat very thinly, especially a small
piece, so it is best to ask your butcher's advice and help.
Putting the beef in the freezer for about 10 minutes should
help to make it a bit more solid and easier to cut.

METRIC/IMPERIAL
100–225 g/4–8 oz fillet
    steak
1 tbsp wine vinegar
3 tbsp olive oil
1 tsp grated onion
1 tsp Dijon mustard
2 anchovy fillets, finely
    chopped, or 1 tsp
    anchovy paste
2 tsp capers, finely chopped
salt and black pepper

Slice the beef very thinly, or have the butcher do
this for you.
    Mix all the remaining ingredients well together
and serve with the meat, or spooned over it.

AMERICAN
¼–½ lb beef tenderloin
1 tbsp wine vinegar
3 tbsp olive oil
1 tsp grated onion
1 tsp Dijon-style mustard
2 anchovy fillets, finely
    chopped, or 1 tsp
    anchovy paste
2 tsp capers, finely chopped
salt and black pepper

PASTA FRITTATA

METRIC/IMPERIAL
225 g/8 oz spaghetti,
    linguine or tagliatelle,
    cooked
1 clove garlic, peeled and
    finely chopped
4 tbsp olive or sunflower oil
4 eggs
25 g/1 oz Cheddar cheese,
    grated
25 g/1 oz Parmesan cheese,
    freshly grated
2 tbsp chopped fresh herbs
    such as parsley, basil and
    oregano
salt and black pepper
oil for frying

Brown the garlic in the olive oil. Mix the spaghetti with the garlic oil.

Beat the eggs in a bowl, and add the two cheeses, the herbs and salt and pepper to taste. Add the pasta, and mix well.

Heat a little oil in a large frying pan and pour in the egg mixture. Cook fairly quickly, until the bottom is browned. Turn the omelette over. When both sides are browned, put on a hot serving dish and serve.

AMERICAN
½ lb spaghetti, linguine or
    tagliatelle, cooked
1 clove garlic, peeled and
    finely chopped
4 tbsp olive or sunflower oil
4 eggs
¼ cup grated Cheddar
    cheese
¼ cup freshly grated
    Parmesan cheese
2 tbsp chopped fresh herbs
    such as parsley, basil and
    oregano
salt and black pepper
oil for frying

CHICKEN DIVAN

A quick and very tasty way of using up leftover chicken or turkey or any white meat.

METRIC/IMPERIAL
about 450 g/1 lb cooked
    chicken meat, sliced
about 450 g/1 lb fresh or
    frozen broccoli
75 g/3 oz Cheddar cheese,
    grated
300-g/10½-oz can
    condensed cream of
    mushroom soup
100 g/4 oz fresh brown
    breadcrumbs
50 g/2 oz butter, melted

Preheat the oven to fairly hot (200°C/400°F/Gas Mark 6).

Thaw frozen broccoli, or lightly cook fresh broccoli, keeping it a little undercooked so it is still firm.

In the bottom of an ovenproof dish lay the broccoli, then the sliced chicken, then the grated cheese. Pour over the undiluted soup. Top with the fresh breadcrumbs and pour the melted butter over.

Bake for about 45 minutes, until the breadcrumbs are crisp and brown and the sauce is bubbling around them.

AMERICAN
about 1 lb cooked chicken
    meat, sliced
about 1 lb fresh or frozen
    broccoli
¾ cup grated Cheddar
    cheese
10½-oz can condensed
    cream of mushroom soup
2 cups fresh brown bread
    crumbs
4 tbsp butter, melted

PORK STROGANOFF

Pork? Stroganoff?? Some mistake, surely? But this is the best name to describe slices of tender pork with mushrooms, onions and sour cream — a party dish for half the price of beef.

METRIC/IMPERIAL
1 pork fillet, about 450 g/
   1 lb
120 ml/4 fl oz apple juice
1 tbsp cider or wine vinegar
2 cloves garlic, peeled and
   crushed
1 bay leaf
1 tbsp chopped fresh thyme
flour for coating
2 medium onions, peeled
   and chopped
a little olive oil and butter
175 g/6 oz mushrooms,
   sliced
150 ml/¼ pint soured
   cream, single cream or
   plain yogurt
salt and black pepper

If you have time, prepare the meat several hours before, and leave it to marinate. Cut off any stringy fat pieces, and slice the pork very thinly crossways. Cover with a mixture of the apple juice, vinegar, garlic, bay leaf and thyme. The actual cooking can be done a little in advance too, and the dish put to keep warm, unlike Boeuf Stroganoff. Or cook it and serve it immediately.

Drain the meat, reserving the marinade, pat it dry and dust with a little flour. Fry the onions in oil until soft and brown. Transfer to dish. Cook the mushrooms until the juice runs, and transfer to the dish. Add a little more oil and some butter to the frying pan, and brown the pork slices, turning them well around and about. Now return the onions and mushrooms to the pan. Stir in the reserved marinade and the cream or yogurt. Heat gently. Add salt and pepper to taste. Test for taste: if the mixture lacks sharpness, add a little lemon juice or more vinegar.

Serve with a plain green salad and potatoes boiled in their skins. Or with a green vegetable, such as broccoli.

AMERICAN
1 pork tenderloin, about 1 lb
½ cup apple juice
1 tbsp cider or wine vinegar
2 cloves garlic, peeled and
   minced
1 bay leaf
1 tbsp chopped fresh thyme
flour for coating
2 medium onions, peeled
   and chopped
a little olive oil and butter
2 cups sliced mushrooms
⅔ cup sour cream, heavy
   cream or plain yogurt
salt and black pepper

PEPPERED STEAK WITH NOODLES

A rapid way of stretching a not very large steak to feed two people. The hot, peppery steak contrasts nicely with the bland noodles.

SERVES 2

METRIC/IMPERIAL
150–175 g/5–6 oz rump steak, trimmed of fat and sliced crossways into strips
2 tbsp cooking oil
2 tsp black or mixed black and green peppercorns, finely crushed in a mortar
1 tsp mild German or French mustard
1 tsp tomato purée
175 ml/6 fl oz soured cream or smetana
salt
175 g/6 oz tagliatelle or flat ribbon noodles
wine or water

AMERICAN
5–6 oz boneless sirloin steak, trimmed of fat and sliced crosswise into strips
2 tbsp cooking oil
2 tsp black or mixed black and green peppercorns, finely crushed in a mortar
1 tsp mild German mustard
1 tsp tomato paste
¾ cup sour cream
salt
6 oz tagliatelle or flat ribbon noodles
wine or water

Dab the steak strips with kitchen paper to dry. Smear with a little oil using the fingertips, then sprinkle with the crushed peppercorns, pressing well in. Whisk the mustard and tomato purée with the cream.

In a large pan of boiling salted water, cook the tagliatelle or noodles till just tender. Drain, run hot water through, then tip into a hot dish with a dribble of oil and keep warm.

In a frying pan, heat the remaining oil and fry the steak strips, shaking frequently to sear both sides. Don't overcook – 2–3 minutes should be enough. They should be just rare inside. Transfer with a spatula to the pasta dish.

Splash a little wine or water into the frying pan, scrape up the little meaty bits and pour in the cream mixture. Let it bubble for 1–2 minutes, stirring well, and pour over the meat and pasta.

Plainly steamed carrots, beans or cauliflower, sprinkled with parsley, go well with this dish.

A useful variant is to substitute strips of lamb's liver for the steak. The peppering makes liver taste mild. Make the sauce with sherry, vermouth or white wine instead of cream, and serve with sauté potatoes and salad.

BAKED FISH PARCELS

Morsels of fish — small steaks, fillets cut into segments or across into strips or "goujons" — wrapped in leaves and baked, look festive, and retain flavour and texture. Grated fresh ginger is a Chinese additive — they claim it "de-fishes" and makes fish taste sweet by contrast — newly popular with nouvelle chefs. Allow 100–150 g/4–5 oz of fish per person, distributed in two parcels each. Choose firm, non-fatty fish like trout, bass or sole, and ask the fishmonger to skin and fillet it, or to slice it into small strips. Keep the trimmings.

METRIC/IMPERIAL

675 g/1½ lb fish steaks or fillets, trimmed and skinned
4 tbsp water
8 large leaves cos or butterleaf lettuce
tiny pinch of sugar
salt and black pepper
bunch of spring onions, finely chopped, or 100 g/4 oz shallots, peeled and finely chopped
1 rounded tsp finely grated fresh ginger
175 ml/6 fl oz dry sherry, dry vermouth or white wine

Preheat the oven to moderate (160°C/325°F/Gas Mark 3).

Simmer the fish trimmings for a few minutes in the water; strain off the stock into a cup.

Open the lettuce leaves in a colander and pour boiling water over till they look limp. Run cold water over briefly, then shake off excess water.

Combine the sugar and salt and pepper to taste in a saucer and smear a trace on each piece of fish. Mix 1 teaspoon of the onions or shallots with the ginger, and sprinkle a little on each piece of fish. Roll the fish in the lettuce leaves to make 12 neat parcels, tucking the ends under.

Combine the strained stock with the sherry, vermouth or wine and the remaining chopped onions or shallots. Bring to the boil in a small pan and reduce to about half by boiling fast. Pour this into a shallow ovenproof dish, arrange the parcels on top and cover with foil. Bake for 5 minutes.

Serve with small steamed new potatoes.

AMERICAN

1½ lb fish steaks or fillets, trimmed and skinned
4 tbsp water
8 large leaves romaine or butterhead lettuce
tiny pinch of sugar
salt and black pepper
bunch of scallions, finely chopped, or ¼ lb shallots, peeled and finely chopped
1 heaping tsp finely grated fresh ginger root
¾ cup dry sherry, dry vermouth or white wine

SOME FRUIT SALADS

Most soft fruits are delicious just as they are, with a dusting of sugar put on several hours before eating, to bring out the flavour and juices. Sugar will also briefly preserve soft fruit like raspberries and strawberries which can go soggy and mouldy in a trice. (Always remove soft fruits from their container as soon as possible, and spread them out in a shallow dish, because even the weight of a few layers of raspberries will soon reduce the ones at the bottom to a mouldy mush.) One other quick tip which is invaluable: warmed liquid honey, or melted set honey, poured over any mixture of solid and citrus fruits will make the salad taste as if it had been basted in liqueurs.

Here are a few suggestions for fruit combinations.

STRAWBERRY AND ORANGE

These two fruits seem to have an affinity: the orange enhances the strawberry taste. Orange juice sprinkled over lightly sugared sliced strawberries is all you need. Or for an interesting treat, add thinly sliced kumquats, the sweet tiny oranges which you eat skin and all.

PEACH AND RASPBERRY

Peaches, raspberry sauce and ice cream are the classic Pêche Melba. But ripe peaches, skinned and with their stone-hollow filled with a sweetened purée of raspberries, will do very well, if not better, without the ice cream to dilute them.

ALMOST VEGETARIAN

Of all the changes which have occurred in our eating habits over the past decade, surely the most unexpected must be the way vegetarianism has shed its old cranky associations and acquired a newly positive image. The "demi-veg" diet is essentially the traditional peasant diet, based on a local staple food, like polenta, backed up by home grown greenstuff and a little animal protein. One reason I have found going demi-veg positively stimulating is that for nine months of the year a large box of seasonal vegetables and other goodies is delivered from a Suffolk farm to my door, once a week. Part of the charm of this arrangement is that I never know what the next box will hold; but the real joy is savouring the vivid flavour of produce almost fresh from the ground, and rediscovering, in an urban context, the old, inevitable rhythm of growth and decay.

PUMPKIN AND ORANGE SOUP

Pumpkin makes a luscious soup. Supermarkets sell cut pumpkin by the pound although whole pumpkins work out cheaper, and the flesh keeps well in a cool place. Use the remaining pumpkin for making chutney.

METRIC/IMPERIAL
675 g/1½ lb pumpkin, peeled, deseeded and diced
25 g/1 oz butter
1 tbsp oil
1 large onion, peeled and chopped
1 clove garlic, peeled and chopped
½ tsp coriander seeds, crushed
½ tsp cumin seeds, crushed
300 ml/½ pint orange juice
600 ml/1 pint vegetable or chicken stock or water
600 ml/1 pint milk
salt and black pepper

Melt the butter with the oil in a large pan. Add the onion, garlic and pumpkin and sweat over low heat, covered, for a few minutes, turning a couple of times. Add the crushed spices, turn for a moment or two, then pour in the orange juice and stock or water. Simmer for 20 minutes, covered, or till the pumpkin is tender.

Purée in a food processor or with a sieve. Add the milk, stir and reheat, seasoning with salt and pepper to taste.

AMERICAN
1½ lb pumpkin, peeled, deseeded and diced
2 tbsp butter
1 tbsp oil
1 large onion, peeled and chopped
1 clove garlic, peeled and chopped
½ tsp coriander seeds, crushed
½ tsp cumin seeds, crushed
1¼ cups orange juice
2½ cups vegetable or chicken stock or water
2½ cups milk
salt and black pepper

ICED TOMATO SOUP

Very refreshing on a hot day, this can be considered as either a soup, or a drink.

METRIC/IMPERIAL
600 ml/1 pint tomato juice
600 ml/1 pint fresh tomato pulp
1 glass dry white wine
grated rind and juice of 2 oranges
salt and black pepper
a little sugar, to taste
150 ml/¼ pint double cream, whipped

Mix the tomato juice, tomato pulp, wine, half the orange rind, the orange juice, and salt and pepper to taste. Blend in a food processor or blender, or mix by hand, making sure the tomatoes are well chopped and mashed. Taste and add more seasoning, and a little sugar if needed.

Chill thoroughly, then serve the soup in cups or bowls, with a spoonful of whipped cream on each and a good dusting of grated orange rind.

AMERICAN
2½ cups tomato juice
2½ cups fresh tomato pulp
1 glass dry white wine
grated rind and juice of 2 oranges
salt and black pepper
a little sugar, to taste
⅔ cup heavy cream, whipped

STUFFED HERRINGS

450 g/1 lb of fish is plenty for 4 people as a main course (or 8 as an appetizer), once they are stuffed. But it's just as well to buy a bit more, if they seem very varied in size. Stuff the largest, and just fry the smallest.

Best of all are the big sprats, big enough to make them worth gutting, but small enough to cook quickly, before the cheese filling melts into the fish. Sardines are very good too, and small herrings, (2 per person) are much quicker to prepare, though you have to be more careful about bones than with the sprats. Once you've got the hang of the sprat de-backboning, life is easy, because that's the only bone you need bother with.

For a party dish, you could make a pretty display of tiny sprats, plain fried, bigger ones stuffed, then a circle of sardines, and then small herrings. Decorate with twisted cucumber slices. Serve with green tagliatelle. Have a bowl of Tzatziki (page 28) with it, or plain yogurt and grated apple.

METRIC/IMPERIAL

675 g/1½ lb small herrings, large sprats or sardines
175 g/6 oz cream cheese
1 tsp horseradish relish
3 tbsp chopped fresh parsley, thyme and tarragon
1 clove garlic, peeled and crushed
salt and black pepper
flour for coating
1 egg
toasted breadcrumbs
oil for deep frying

To prepare herrings: cut off the head and tail. Slit down the side and remove the guts. Turn over, and press down hard with the blade of a knife to flatten. Turn over again and remove the backbone. With the flat of the knife, or tweezers, remove any long bones left on either side at the head end of the fish. Trim off small bones at the upper edges. Turn over and cut off the central fin.

To prepare sprats: cut off the head and tail. Slit down the side, scraping out any innards. Turn the sprat over and press down flat, pressing hard with the side of the knife against the backbone, from the head end. Turn over again and pull out the backbone, which will come away with no trouble.

Mix the cheese with the horseradish, herbs,

AMERICAN

1½ lb small herrings, large smelts or sardines
6 oz (about ¾ cup) cream cheese
1 tsp horseradish relish or prepared horseradish
3 tbsp chopped fresh parsley, thyme and tarragon
1 clove garlic, peeled and minced
salt and black pepper
flour for coating
1 egg
toasted breadcrumbs
oil for deep frying

garlic, and salt and pepper to taste.

Spread a spoonful of the cheese mixture down the centre of each fish and then fold it over to reform a fish shape. Flour. Beat the egg in a shallow bowl. Put a heap of breadcrumbs into a similar bowl next to it. Dip each fish into the egg, then the breadcrumbs to coat it thoroughly, and then lay out on a dish. (This is a messy business.)

Heat oil, either for deep frying or shallow frying. If shallow frying, cook for 2–3 minutes on each side, in two or three batches if necessary, so that the fish don't touch. Finally throw in any little sprats, floured. Drain on kitchen paper.

PARMIGIANA

A classic, substantial Italian dish based on aubergines.

Preheat the oven to moderately hot (190°C/375°F/Gas Mark 5).

Make the tomato sauce by softening the onion in a little olive oil. Add the celery, tomatoes, parsley, and salt and pepper to taste. Cook until the vegetables are quite soft, and the sauce reduced.

Lightly flour the aubergine slices. Fry gently until browned in oil. Drain and put to one side.

Oil the bottom of an ovenproof dish, and put in a layer of aubergine. Sprinkle on a little salt and pepper, then cover with a layer of mozzarella slices and a little tomato sauce. Add more aubergine, and so on. Sprinkle the top with Parmesan, and put to bake for about 30 minutes.

METRIC/IMPERIAL
900 g/2 lb aubergines, sliced
1 small onion, peeled and chopped
olive oil for frying
1 stick celery, chopped
450 g/1 lb tomatoes, peeled and chopped or 400-g/14-oz can tomatoes, broken up, with their juice
chopped parsley
salt and black pepper
flour for coating
225 g/8 oz mozzarella or Gruyère cheese, thinly sliced
50 g/2 oz Parmesan or Cheddar cheese, freshly grated

AMERICAN
2 lb eggplants, sliced
1 small onion, peeled and chopped
olive oil for frying
1 stalk celery, chopped
1 lb tomatoes, peeled and chopped or 14-oz can tomatoes, broken up, with their juice
chopped parsley
salt and black pepper
flour for coating
½ lb mozzarella or Gruyère cheese thinly sliced
½ cup freshly grated Parmesan or Cheddar cheese

VEGETABLE FRITTERS
(Fritto Misto)

This could be looked on as a leftovers dish, and in fact, most cooked vegetables can be used in this. But it is most delicious and nutritious made with fresh, uncooked vegetables, which retain some of their crispness.

METRIC/IMPERIAL

a choice of:
aubergine, sliced
cauliflower, separated into
　little florets
firm tomatoes, halved if
　large
courgettes, sliced
small button mushrooms
Jerusalem artichokes,
　peeled and parboiled
turnips, peeled and cut into
　small pieces
oil for deep frying

BATTER
100 g/4 oz flour
pinch of salt
2 tbsp light olive or
　sunflower oil
150 ml/¼ pint lukewarm
　water
1 egg white

The aubergine slices should be sprinkled with salt and left for 30 minutes, to remove any bitterness. Cauliflower is particularly good frittered, as it goes soft and creamy on the inside.

To make the batter: sift the flour and salt into a bowl, stir in the oil, and add the water gradually, beating all to a smooth paste. Leave for 1–2 hours if possible. Before using the batter, add the stiffly beaten egg white.

Heat oil in a deep fryer, or in a frying pan for shallow frying. It is hot enough when a blob of batter sizzles and coagulates on being dropped in. Dip the pieces of vegetable in the batter and lift out in one spoon, scraping off excess batter with another. If you are using two or three different kinds of vegetable, keep them separate, and fry all of one kind in one batch so that they will have the same cooking time. Don't overfill the pan, to make sure the pieces don't stick to each other. When golden brown, turn over to cook the vegetables through. The oil should not be too hot, because raw vegetables need a little time to cook – less time, obviously, if already cooked. Drain on paper towels.

AMERICAN

a choice of:
eggplant, sliced
cauliflower, separated into
　little florets
firm tomatoes, halved if
　large
zucchini, sliced
small button mushrooms
Jerusalem artichokes,
　peeled and parboiled
turnips, peeled and cut into
　small pieces
oil for deep frying

BATTER
¾ cup flour
pinch of salt
2 tbsp light olive or
　sunflower oil
⅔ cup lukewarm water
1 egg white

RISI E BISI

Frozen peas (or even canned petits pois) can be used instead of fresh ones, in which case they must be added near the end of the cooking or they will disintegrate. This is a simple but delicious rice dish from Venice.

METRIC/IMPERIAL
1 small onion, peeled and
    chopped
25 g/1 oz butter
50 g/2 oz cooked ham or
    prosciutto, chopped
350 g/12 oz long-grain or
    easy-cook rice
350 g/12 oz shelled fresh or
    frozen peas
about 900 ml/1½ pints
    chicken stock
salt and black pepper
25 g/1 oz Parmesan or
    Cheddar cheese, freshly
    grated
extra butter to finish

Soften the onion in the butter. Add the ham and then the rice and fresh peas. Stir around. Add the stock and season with salt. Bring to the boil, then turn the heat very low, put a lid on the saucepan and leave to cook for 15–17 minutes.

If using frozen peas, heat them in a little water, drain and add them to the rice halfway through cooking, stirring them in gently with a fork. (Canned petits pois are drained and forked in in the same way.)

Fluff up the rice with a fork, and stir in a generous amount of chopped butter, the grated cheese, and pepper to taste.

By leaving out the ham, and substituting vegetable stock, this can very easily be rendered meatless.

AMERICAN
1 small onion, peeled and
    chopped
2 tbsp butter
⅓ cup chopped cooked
    ham or prosciutto
2 cups long-grain rice
2½ cups shelled fresh or
    frozen peas
about 4 cups chicken stock
salt and black pepper
¼ cup freshly grated
    Parmesan or Cheddar
    cheese
extra butter to finish

SMOKED HADDOCK SOUFFLÉ

A soufflé is the most attractive way to make something of leftover smoked fish. You could also use white fish, but in that case substitute Parmesan for the parsley. Lady Maclean relates that Sir Charles Mendl, the enormously wealthy bon vivant, used to give lunch parties in the 30s in Paris where the menu invariably consisted of Haddock Soufflé followed by Shepherd's Pie, two dishes he regarded as the ideal background to fine wine. She does not specify which wines, but I find a modest claret slips down very pleasantly.

METRIC/IMPERIAL

about 225 g/8 oz smoked haddock fillet, cooked
25 g/1 oz butter
2 tbsp flour
300 ml/½ pint hot milk
1 tbsp grated onion
2 tbsp finely chopped parsley
4 egg yolks
5 egg whites
salt and black pepper

AMERICAN

about ½ lb smoked haddock fillet (finnan haddie) cooked
2 tbsp butter
2½ tbsp flour
1¼ cups hot milk
1 tbsp grated onion
2 tbsp finely chopped parsley
4 egg yolks
5 egg whites
salt and black pepper

Preheat the oven to fairly hot (200°C/400°F/Gas Mark 6).

Flake the fish, discarding any skin and bones. Set aside.

Make the basic white sauce by melting the butter in a saucepan, stirring in the flour, then adding the hot milk gradually. Stir over low heat till the mixture thickens. Continue cooking, stirring, for a couple of minutes, then remove from the heat and stir in the onion, parsley and fish.

Whisk the egg yolks and add to the fish mixture. Beat the whites till stiff enough to stand in peaks, and fold gently but thoroughly into the fish mixture.

Pour into a greased soufflé dish, or small oval casserole, and bake for 5 minutes. Then without opening the oven door, turn the heat down one notch and bake for another 20 minutes. The soufflé should be well risen and just browned on top.

Serve at once on hot plates, with green beans, spinach or broccoli.

BROCCOLI WITH PASTA AND NUT SAUCE

A substantial vegetarian main course. Ground nuts always have more flavour if you buy whole nuts; skin, toast lightly and grind as needed.

Either use one big serving dish, or serve the broccoli separately. Heat the dishes in a moderate oven, so that they are warm and ready, as the meal does not take long to cook. Pasta is more appetizing served piping hot, on hot plates.

SERVES 4–6

METRIC/IMPERIAL

900 g/2 lb broccoli, broken into florets, stalks trimmed and sliced
salt and black pepper
450 g/1 lb rigatoni or macaroni
3 cloves garlic, peeled and chopped
1 small fresh chilli, chopped, or ½ tsp chilli powder
1 tbsp sesame seeds
3 tbsp olive oil
1 tbsp chopped parsley

NUT SAUCE

25 g/1 oz butter
450 g/1 lb tomatoes, peeled and chopped
300 ml/½ pint single cream
175 g/6 oz cashew nuts or blanched almonds, ground

Put the broccoli to boil in a little salted water or steam until barely tender. At the same time, cook the pasta in a large quantity of boiling salted water; when ready, drain the pasta.

Meanwhile, fry the garlic, chilli and sesame seeds in the olive oil. Stir in the parsley. Drain the broccoli, pour over the mixture and keep hot.

Make the sauce by heating the butter and quickly frying the tomatoes. Stir in the cream and nuts and cook for 2–3 minutes.

Serve the broccoli surrounded by the pasta, with the sauce poured over.

AMERICAN

2 lb broccoli, broken into florets, stalks trimmed and sliced
salt and black pepper
1 lb rigatoni or macaroni
3 cloves garlic, peeled and chopped
1 small fresh chili pepper, chopped, or ½ tsp chili powder
1 tbsp sesame seeds
3 tbsp olive oil
1 tbsp chopped parsley

NUT SAUCE

2 tbsp butter
1 lb tomatoes, peeled and chopped
1¼ cups heavy cream
1½ cups ground cashew nuts or almonds

COURGETTES WITH DILL

You can use any amount of courgettes — it just depends on
what else you are serving, and the size of dish you want to use.
These are easiest cooked on top of the stove.

METRIC/IMPERIAL
675 g/1½ lb courgettes
a little butter
a good handful of fresh dill,
   chopped
salt and black pepper
1–2 tbsp water

Chop off the courgette stalks. Slice in half
lengthways, and then cut each half across
diagonally. (This is just to make a more interesting
shape than the usual discs, and also because it
seems to make them taste better, but that could be
an illusion.)

Heat a little butter in a flameproof dish or pan.
Put in the courgettes, and turn in the butter. Add
the dill and salt and pepper to taste. Turn the
courgettes over again. (A slotted spoon is the most
useful implement here.) Now add the water, put
on the lid, turn the heat down low, and let the
courgettes stew in their own juice.

Serve with one soft-boiled egg per person, to
make a meal.

AMERICAN
1½ lb zucchini
a little butter
a good handful of fresh dill,
   chopped
salt and black pepper
1–2 tbsp water

MUSHROOM PIE

This is a particularly luscious pie and makes an elegant and substantial main dish. Although the bacon does add to the taste, it can be left out to make a vegetarian meal. A very few dried porcini, soaked first, will perk up the mushroom flavour wonderfully.

SERVES 6

Preheat the oven to hot (220°C/425°F/Mark 7).

Soften the onion, garlic and parsley in a mixture of half the butter and the olive oil. Add the bacon and cook till the fat runs out.

Add the mushroms (and porcini, if used) and let them cook gently for a few minutes. Add the thyme, and salt and the pepper to taste. Sprinkle over the crumbled stock cube and flour and mix around, then pour over the milk. Stir well and bring the mixture to the boil. Cook for a minute or two further, then take the pan off the heat and let the contents cool a little. Now add the eggs, mixing them in well one by one, and the cheeses.

Divide the pastry in half; roll out one half and use to line a 25 cm/10 in flan or quiche dish. Fill with the mushroom mixture. Roll out the other piece of pastry to make a lid. Moisten all around the edge with water and cover the pie, pinching the edges together tightly to seal. With any little bits of pastry over, make four ovals and a little knob or curled ball, to garnish the centre of the pie, like a flower and leaves. Glaze with beaten egg.

Put into the hot oven and bake for 20 minutes, then turn the heat down to moderately hot (190°C/375°F/Gas Mark 5). Bake for a further 15 minutes at least, to make sure the pastry is well cooked under the pie. If the surface seems to be browning too much, cover with foil or greaseproof/wax paper. (This pie can be left for a while in the oven without coming to harm, as long as the heat is turned down a little more.)

METRIC/IMPERIAL

350 g/12 oz button mushrooms, sliced
1 small onion, peeled and chopped
1 clove garlic, peeled and finely chopped
a good handful of parsley, chopped
25 g/1 oz butter
2 tbsp olive oil
50 g/2 oz green bacon, chopped (optional)
1 tsp chopped fresh thyme
salt and black pepper
1 stock cube, crumbled
25 g/1 oz flour
225 ml/8 fl oz milk
3 eggs
1 egg yolk
50 g/2 oz Parmesan or Cheddar cheese, freshly grated
50 g/2 oz Emmenthal cheese, cubed
rough puff pastry made from 225 g/8 oz flour and 175 g/6 oz fat (see page 20), or a packet of frozen puff pastry, thawed
beaten egg to glaze

AMERICAN

¾ lb button mushrooms, sliced
1 small onion, peeled and chopped
1 clove garlic, peeled and finely chopped
a good handful of parsley, chopped
2 tbsp butter
2 tbsp olive oil
⅓ cup chopped bacon (optional)
1 tsp chopped fresh thyme
salt and black pepper
1 bouillon cube, crumbled
3 tbsp flour
1 cup milk
3 eggs
1 egg yolk
½ cup freshly grated Parmesan or Cheddar cheese
⅓ cup cubed Emmenthal or Swiss cheese
rough puff pastry made from 1¾ cups flour and 1½ sticks fat (see page 20), or a package of frozen puff pastry, thawed
beaten egg to glaze

GRILLED FISH WITH SALSA VERDE OR ROUILLE

Fish steaks, brushed with oil and grilled/broiled are good eating when the fish is fresh and firm. Serve one of these two lusty sauces, rapidly made in a processor, with the fish and a few steamed potatoes.

METRIC/IMPERIAL
4 large or 8 small fish steaks
2 tbsp olive or safflower oil
1–2 drops sesame oil
salt and black pepper

SALSA VERDE
a good handful of parsley
1 clove garlic, peeled
10 capers
2 anchovy fillets
1 slice bread, moistened
   with wine vinegar and
   squeezed
olive oil

ROUILLE
2 tbsp olive oil
1 medium onion, peeled
   and finely chopped
1 clove garlic, peeled and
   finely chopped
200-g/7-oz can pimientoes,
   drained
1 red chilli, deseeded

For the salsa verde: put the parsley, garlic, capers, anchovies and bread in a food processor and blend in a couple of short bursts. Or chop and pound to a paste in a mortar. Add the olive oil, blending or stirring to make a thick sauce.

For the rouille: in a small pan heat the oil, add the onion, cover and soften over low heat for 3–4 minutes. Add the garlic and heat through 1 minute longer. Process together with the pimientoes and chilli until smooth. Set aside for a few minutes to develop the flavours.

Pat the fish steaks dry on both sides and brush over with the oil. Rub in seasoning to taste. Sear the steaks rapidly on both sides under the grill/broiler, then lower the heat or move the fish further away, and continue cooking for approximately 2 minutes on each side or till the flesh is flaky and opaque. Serve on hot plates with the sauce in a bowl.

AMERICAN
4 large or 8 small fish steaks
2 tbsp olive or safflower oil
1–2 drops sesame oil
salt and black pepper

SALSA VERDE
a good handful of parsley
1 clove garlic, peeled
10 capers
2 anchovy fillets
1 slice bread, moistened
   with wine vinegar and
   squeezed
olive oil

ROUILLE
2 tbsp olive oil
1 medium onion, peeled
   and finely chopped
1 clove garlic, peeled and
   finely chopped
7-oz can pimientoes,
   drained
1 small red chili pepper,
   deseeded

GRATIN OF JERUSALEM ARTICHOKES AND SMOKED HADDOCK

Jerusalem artichokes, the knobbly root vegetable which looks a bit like a potato, has a striking affinity with fish. You could use any white fish here, or salmon, but a mixture of smoked and fresh haddock makes a not too strong-tasting combination.
Look for the smoothest artichokes, as they do vary.
(People say that they get more knobbly later in the season.)

METRIC/IMPERIAL
450 g/1 lb Jerusalem artichokes
a little lemon juice or vinegar
225 g/8 oz smoked haddock fillet
225 g/8 oz white fish fillet (haddock, cod, etc.)
a little milk and water
1 bay leaf
50 g/2 oz butter
25 g/1 oz flour
about 300 ml/½ pint milk
50 g/2 oz Cheddar cheese, grated
50 g/2 oz fresh breadcrumbs
salt and black pepper

If the artichokes are very knobbly, steam or boil them first till barely tender, then peel and slice them. Otherwise, peel and slice them, putting them in water made acid with lemon juice or vinegar to keep them white. Boil in a very little water with a little butter for about 8 minutes; when tender drain.

Meanwhile put the fish to poach in a little milk and water, with the bay leaf. Drain, reserving the liquid, and take any bones or skin out of the fish.

Make a sauce with half of the butter, the flour, the reserved fish poaching liquid, and the milk. Stir in half the grated cheese.

Put the artichokes in the bottom of an ovenproof dish. Cover them with a layer of fish and pour over the sauce. Mix the remaining cheese with the breadcrumbs and a little salt and pepper and spread over the top. Cut the remaining butter into little pieces and dot over the top. Bake until the top is brown and crisp.

✎ This can be made into a more elaborate dish by putting the artichoke and fish combination in a pastry case (previously baked blind). Hard-boil 3 eggs, cut each in quarters, and lay them on top of the fish like the spokes of a wheel. Sprinkle paprika over.

AMERICAN
1 lb Jerusalem artichokes
a little lemon juice or vinegar
½ lb smoked haddock fillet (finnan haddie)
½ lb white fish fillet (haddock, cod, etc.)
a little milk and water
1 bay leaf
4 tbsp butter
2 tbsp flour
about 1¼ cups milk
½ cup grated Cheddar cheese
1 cup fresh bread crumbs
salt and black pepper

ENGLISH RATATOUILLE
OR VEGETABLE RAGOUT

This has become such a glory and standby of our family cooking that aggrieved members say: "What, no rat?" if they come for a weekend and find it missing. A ratatouille is basically just a mixture of vegetables all cooked together; the delicious French version is very similar to the following, except that it has aubergines/eggplants in it.

This concoction originated in days when aubergine was rare and expensive. We even tried making it without the green pepper, but decided that it was necessary. Of course, you can experiment and use whatever vegetables are available, but this combination seems to be particularly successful.

The amounts are rather approximate. In the courgette season, they tend to predominate.

METRIC/IMPERIAL
4–5 courgettes
2–3 carrots, peeled
4 tbsp sunflower or olive oil
2 large onions, peeled and sliced
1 green pepper, deseeded and sliced
400-g/14-oz can tomatoes
1 bay leaf
thyme
1 clove garlic, peeled and crushed (optional)
salt and black pepper

AMERICAN
4–5 zucchini
2–3 carrots, peeled
4 tbsp sunflower or olive oil
2 large onions, peeled and sliced
1 green pepper, deseeded and sliced
14-oz can tomatoes
1 bay leaf
thyme
1 clove garlic, peeled and minced (optional)
salt and black pepper

Slice some courgettes in rounds, and some in other shapes. If the carrots are small and new, chop them, but if they are big and old, slice them very thinly, as they seem to take a long time to soften.

Heat the oil in a heavy saucepan or large frying pan, and put in the vegetables in order, turning and cooking them a little and not worrying if they brown: first the onions, then the pepper, then the carrots and then the courgettes. Let them cook on a medium heat, turning, for about 10 minutes.

Now add the tomatoes with their juice and all the seasonings. Turn the heat down and let the mixture simmer. Make sure the carrots are well covered. Cook for at least 20 minutes, stirring occasionally, or until all the vegetables are cooked and the sauce is thickish and tomatoey. If it is too thick, add a little water.

You can serve this hot or cold. It will keep very well for several days, and can be reheated.

ARTICHOKE HEARTS WITH BROAD BEANS

A sophisticated cooked salad, good as an appetizer, this is best made with small fresh artichokes, though the beans used can be frozen to save time.

METRIC/IMPERIAL
4–6 globe artichokes, depending on size
juice of 2 lemons
4 tbsp olive oil
3 cloves garlic, peeled and chopped
450 g/1 lb frozen broad beans
150 ml/¼ pint water
salt and black pepper
1 tbsp finely chopped fresh herbs such as parsley, fennel or oregano

AMERICAN
4–6 globe artichokes, depending on size
juice of 2 lemons
4 tbsp olive oil
3 cloves garlic, peeled and chopped
1 lb frozen lima beans
⅔ cup water
salt and black pepper
1 tbsp finely chopped fresh herbs such as parsley, fennel or oregano

Only the artichoke bottoms are required. To make these more easily accessible, throw the whole artichokes into a large pan of rapidly boiling water, along with the squeezed lemon skins, and cook for 10–12 minutes, or until just tender. Remove, refresh under cold running water, then pull the leaves off the bottoms in a clump and scrape off the fuzzy choke with a spoon. Trim off any stalk, and cut the bottoms across into thick slices.

Put the artichoke slices with the lemon juice, oil, garlic and beans into a wide shallow pan. Heat gently, partly covered, till the beans are thawed. Add the water, bring rapidly to the boil, then reduce the heat and simmer for 10–15 minutes, shaking the pan occasionally. Season to taste with salt and pepper, sprinkle with the herbs, and leave to cool. Serve at room temperature.

IMPERIAL
POTATO SALAD

A little good steak, cooked rare and cut into strips, makes a sprightly salad and goes much further mixed with cooked potatoes and a soured cream dressing sharpened with horseradish.

METRIC/IMPERIAL
450 g/1 lb waxy potatoes
150–175 g/5–6 oz piece
 fillet or rump steak
5 tbsp olive oil
salt and black pepper
6 spring onions, finely
 chopped
1½ tbsp wine vinegar
175 ml/6 fl oz soured cream
1 scant tbsp creamed
 horseradish
2 tbsp finely chopped
 parsley, fennel or celery
 leaves

Put the potatoes to cook in a large pan of boiling water for 10–15 minutes, or till tender when pierced with a fork. Drain, and leave covered while you cook the steak.

Trim off any fat from the steak, brush both sides with ½ tablespoon oil and grill/broil or fry: sear both sides quickly, then lower the heat and cook for 2–3 minutes on each side, turning once.

Peel the potatoes and slice thickly into a good-looking dish. Sprinkle over salt and freshly ground pepper and the onions. Mix the remaining oil with the vinegar, sprinkle over the potatoes and turn gently with salad servers to mix.

Slice the steak into thin short strips across the grain, discarding any gristle or fat. Add to the salad, with any pan juices. Whisk the cream with the horseradish and herbs and add to the salad, forking and turning lightly again to distribute evenly.

Leave for an hour, if possible, to allow flavours to develop, and serve at room temperature with a crisp coleslaw containing some apple, or one small sugarheart lettuce per person.

AMERICAN
1 lb boiling potatoes
5–6 oz piece beef
 tenderloin or boneless
 sirloin steak
5 tbsp olive oil
salt and black pepper
6 scallions, finely chopped
1½ tbsp wine vinegar
¾ cup sour cream
1 scant tbsp creamed
 horseradish or prepared
 horseradish
2 tbsp finely chopped
 parsley, fennel or celery
 leaves

PEPERONATA

The best of all pepper recipes. There are two ways of making it, either in the oven, (which takes the longest but to my mind is the best) or in a pan on top of the stove. Here first is the recipe given to me in Italian by an Italian teacher, as a dictation, enunciating every tasty syllable with loving gusto.

METRIC/IMPERIAL

4 peppers of mixed colours or all red, cored, deseeded and roughly chopped
3 onions, peeled and sliced
1 large clove garlic, peeled and chopped
salt and black pepper
3 tbsp olive oil
450 g/1 lb tomatoes, chopped or 400-g/14-oz can tomatoes, broken up, with their juice

Preheat the oven to hot (220°C/425°F/Gas Mark 7).

Put the peppers and onions in an ovenproof dish. Sprinkle over the garlic and salt and pepper to taste. Pour on the olive oil. Add the tomatoes. Mix, then cover and cook in the oven for about 20 minutes.

Take the lid off, stir the vegetables and continue cooking until the peppers begin to blacken a little around the edges. Stir the vegetables again. When thoroughly cooked and tender, even a little browned, eat hot or cold.

Serve with sausages and baked potatoes. Any leftovers go well as a snack with French bread – or with cheese.

The quicker version is to char the peppers under the grill/broiler and peel off the skins before chopping. Cook with the onions and garlic in the oil in a heavy frying pan or saucepan until the onions are softened, then add the tomatoes and cook uncovered until all are tender.

AMERICAN

4 sweet peppers of mixed colors or all red, cored, deseeded and roughly chopped
3 onions, peeled and sliced
1 large clove garlic, peeled and chopped
salt and black pepper
3 tbsp olive oil
1 lb tomatoes, chopped or 14-oz can tomatoes, broken up, with their juice

QUICK APPLE FLAN

METRIC/IMPERIAL
450 g/1 lb dessert apples, peeled, cored and sliced
100 g/4 oz butter, melted
175 g/6 oz flour
3 tbsp demerara or soft brown sugar
2 tsp cornflour
2 tbsp double cream

AMERICAN
1 lb dessert apples, peeled, cored and sliced
1 stick butter, melted
1¼ cups flour
3 tbsp light brown sugar
2 tsp cornstarch
2 tbsp heavy cream

Preheat the oven to fairly hot (200°C/400°F/Gas Mark 6). Grease an 18–20 cm/7–8 in flan or quiche dish.

Mix the melted butter into the flour with a knife, and quickly form into a dough. Press into the flan dish, spreading it over with your fingertips.

Mix the apples with the sugar and cornflour, and fill the dish, spreading out evenly. Bake for 30–40 minutes, until the apples are browned and the pastry cooked.

Spoon the cream over, then return to the oven to bake for a few more minutes for the cream to warm. Serve hot.

APRICOT MOUSSE

A winter dessert, this is a deliberately light and not oversweet version.

METRIC/IMPERIAL
225 g/8 oz dried apricots, soaked overnight
grated rind and juice of 1 lemon
1 tbsp or more honey
150 ml/¼ pint plain yogurt or lightly whipped cream
15 g/½ oz powdered gelatine
4 tbsp water
2 egg whites
flaked almonds

AMERICAN
½ lb (about 2 cups) dried apricots, soaked overnight
grated rind and juice of 1 lemon
1 tbsp or more honey
⅔ cup plain yogurt or lightly whipped cream
4 tsp unflavored gelatin
4 tbsp water
2 egg whites
sliced almonds

Cook the apricots gently in their soaking water till soft. Purée in blender with the lemon rind and juice. Stir in the honey, adding more to taste if desired, then mix in the yogurt or cream.

Dissolve the gelatine in the water. Add to the apricot mixture. Whisk the egg whites until stiff and fold in.

Leave to set, and serve decorated with almonds.

You can omit the gelatine, and whisk the egg whites straight in, to make a soft creamy pudding.

THE WHOLE STORY

Anyone who wants to eat healthily and well without breaking the bank should familiarize themselves with the wide range of dried beans, grains and cereals which come under the heading of wholefoods. The best reason for trying them is that they are such interesting foods; keeping a selection on hand is an easy way of adding all sorts of pleasing textures and earthy flavours to your diet. That they are good for you is a nice plus, though if you are vegetarian they will also be nutritionally important.

Their flavour always seems to benefit from pungent additions, a scatter of fresh herbs, or a squeeze of lemon juice and fresh coriander. Most dried beans and peas make excellent salads; it always makes sense to cook more than you will need for one meal, so that the remainder can be anointed with a highly seasoned dressing while still warm.

TABBOULEH WITH COUSCOUS

As this is a good party dish, for a buffet, this recipe is in large quantities — enough for about 8 people, or more, if there are many other things to eat. But it is also a very healthy fresh meal for any day, with garlic or pitta bread or, best of all, that rather gooey, many-grained loaf you can sometimes buy.

Fresh mint is essential, so if you make this in winter, search it out. There should be lots of it in the dish, and parsley too. Lemons vary considerably in their juiciness. I have made it with 3 very juicy lemons, and found it very sour, so it's best to add more lemon juice before serving, if the dish seems too bland, rather than swamp it irrecoverably early on. If spring onions are unavailable, very finely chopped small leeks will do.

Tabbouleh is of course usually made with bulgur.

SERVES ABOUT 8

METRIC/IMPERIAL
225 g/8 oz couscous
300 ml/½ pint boiling water
450 g/1 lb tomatoes, peeled and chopped
2 bunches spring onions or 225 g/8 oz leeks, finely chopped
large bunch of parsley, finely chopped
large bunch of mint, finely chopped
grated rind and juice of 2–3 lemons
½ tsp ground cumin
6 tbsp olive oil
salt and black pepper

Put the couscous into a big salad bowl. Pour on the boiling water, and leave for 10 minutes for the grains to swell.

Add all the remaining ingredients to the couscous and stir around. Leave for about 2 hours for all the flavours to mingle.

Before serving, taste for seasoning, and add salt or pepper, or a little more lemon juice if needed. Fluff up the salad with a fork, and serve with lettuce and black olives.

Tabbouleh is originally a Lebanese dish, but it is found all along the Mediterranean. Much eaten in Paris, too (where it is spelt Tabboulé).

AMERICAN
1⅓ cups couscous
1¼ cups boiling water
1 lb tomatoes, peeled and chopped
2 bunches scallions or ½ lb leeks, finely chopped
large bunch of parsley, finely chopped
large bunch of mint, finely chopped
grated rind and juice of 2–3 lemons
½ tsp ground cumin
6 tbsp olive oil
salt and black pepper

ASPARAGUS RISOTTO

A delicate and subtle risotto, serve this on its own as a first course, or to accompany ham, or slices of pork fillet/tenderloin. Drink Marsala or a dry sherry with this.

METRIC/IMPERIAL
225 g/8 oz asparagus, trimmed fresh or canned
1 onion, peeled and chopped
50 g/2 oz butter
225 g/8 oz Italian arborio rice or easy-cook rice
120 ml/4 fl oz white wine
vegetable or chicken stock or water
salt and black pepper
50 g/2 oz Parmesan or Cheddar cheese, freshly grated
a good squeeze of lemon juice

AMERICAN
½ lb asparagus, trimmed fresh or canned
1 onion, peeled and chopped
4 tbsp butter
1⅓ cups Italian arborio rice
½ cup white wine
vegetable or chicken stock or water
salt and black pepper
½ cup freshly grated Parmesan or Cheddar cheese
a good squeeze of lemon juice

If using fresh asparagus, cook it in a little boiling water until just tender; drain, reserving the cooking liquid. Chop the asparagus, trimming off any tough pieces. If using canned asparagus, drain, reserving the juice, and chop the asparagus.

In a saucepan, gently soften the onion in half the butter. Add the rice and stir around until well coated in butter. Add the wine, and let it bubble for a few minutes.

Add the asparagus liquid to vegetable or light chicken stock or water to make 500 ml/18 fl oz/2¼ cups of liquid. Add to the rice with the asparagus and a little salt, stir and bring to the boil. Turn down the heat to its lowest, cover the pan and leave to cook for 20 minutes.

If the risotto is too liquid, take off the lid and leave to cook for a little longer. Cover with a tea-cloth/dish towel to absorb the moisture.

Fork up the risotto, which should be creamy and moist. Stir in the remaining butter, the cheese, a little pepper and a good squeeze of lemon.

To cook pork fillet/tenderloin to serve with the risotto: slice it into 1 cm/½ in medallions. Cover both sides with a marinade of crushed garlic, black pepper or green peppercorns, and lemon juice. Fry in a little butter, turning once.

RICE WITH CHICKEN LIVERS AND FENNEL

This is a very tasty, simple dish, exceedingly useful when you don't know exactly when guests will arrive to eat it. It keeps warm for ages without harm, and gets tastier. Serve it hot or cold. This makes enough for 4 for the main course, or 6–9 people as a first course.

METRIC/IMPERIAL
100 g/4 oz chicken livers
2 tbsp olive or sunflower oil
1 large onion, peeled and
    finely chopped
350 g/12 oz long-grain rice
900 ml/1½ pints water
1 bay leaf
2 fennel roots, coarsely
    chopped
salt and black pepper
freshly grated Parmesan or
    Cheddar cheese to serve

AMERICAN
¼ lb chicken livers
2 tbsp olive or sunflower oil
1 large onion, peeled and
    finely chopped
2 cups long-grain rice
3¾ cups water
1 bay leaf
2 fennel bulbs, coarsely
    chopped
salt and black pepper
freshly grated Parmesan or
    Cheddar cheese to serve

Use a heavy-bottomed saucepan or large frying pan. Chop the chicken livers, removing any little stringy bits. Heat the oil and add the onion, cooking for a few minutes on a medium heat. Add the rice and stir around well, until the rice grains begin to turn white and opaque. Add the chicken livers, stir, and then add the water, bay leaf, chopped fennel (reserving the feathery leaves) and salt and pepper to taste. Turn up the heat and bring to the boil, then turn down the heat to its very lowest and put the lid on the saucepan. Leave to cook for 20 minutes until just tender.

Serve garnished with the fennel leaves. Hand the cheese around separately in a bowl.

 Chickens have lost their hearts and livers in supermarkets, but the livers can easily be bought frozen in tubs, or from butchers. They are strong-tasting and tender, so a little goes a long way. If you have to buy a larger quantity than you need for one dish, don't worry; they will keep for several days in the refrigerator, and can be used to fill crêpes, added to stuffings, bolognese sauce, or to make a sauce on their own, for chicken.

■ If you haven't got chicken livers, this dish is very good with just the onion, cheese and fennel.

■ If you haven't got fennel, this dish is very good with just the onion, cheese and livers. (Add a little more, if you have some.)

■ If you have stock, you can use it instead of water, but this dish is fine made with water.

HOT LENTIL SALAD

Green lentils don't need soaking, and only take about half an hour to cook. They hold their shape, and don't turn to mush like the little orange lentils. (Brown lentils are unskinned orange ones — you can use brown ones for this dish too.)

METRIC/IMPERIAL
225 g/8 oz green lentils
salt and black pepper
1 onion, peeled and finely
  sliced
2 rashers streaky bacon, cut
  into fine shreds
butter for frying
1 tbsp lemon juice
3 tbsp olive oil
chopped parsley

AMERICAN
½ lb (about 1¼ cups) green
  lentils
salt and black pepper
1 onion, peeled and finely
  sliced
2 slices bacon, cut into fine
  shreds
butter for frying
1 tbsp lemon juice
3 tbsp olive oil
chopped parsley

Put the lentils to cook in boiling salted water for about 30 minutes.

Meanwhile, fry the onion and bacon in a little butter. Keep warm.

In a serving bowl, mix the lemon juice, olive oil and black pepper to taste. When the lentils are cooked, drain them and add to the dressing. Add the chopped parsley, onion and bacon. Mix and serve hot, although this can also be served cold if you like.

■ A variation of this is to omit the bacon, add 1 teaspoon of ground cumin to the dressing. Sprinkle with paprika.

POLENTA PIE WITH MUSHROOMS

The mixture of semolina (coarse ground durum wheat) and maize meal (polenta) makes a light and moist golden interior, with a slightly crunchy outside. The pie case is baked separately, in a circle, to be filled when cooked. Fillings can vary, as you please, from chicken to seafood to kidneys, but this is a vegetarian version.

Italian polenta is slightly more granular than the usual yellow cornmeal, but whichever you use it's an interesting alternative to pasta and rice dishes. Also, you don't need to slave over a hot stove at the last minute, juggling pasta *and* sauce. This is tucked away in the oven until the moment of serving. But don't make it in advance, because the polenta will set almost solid.

The circular case can be made in a ring mould, or simply put the mixture to bake in a deep ovenproof dish, pressing it up around the edge and leaving the centre free to be filled with mushrooms.

METRIC/IMPERIAL
75 g/3 oz semolina
75 g/3 oz yellow cornmeal
salt
600 ml/1 pint milk
40 g/1½ oz butter, cut into pieces
50 g/2 oz Parmesan or Cheddar cheese, freshly grated
2 egg yolks
freshly grated nutmeg
1 tbsp toasted breadcrumbs

AMERICAN
¾ cup semolina flour
¾ cup yellow cornmeal
salt
2½ cups milk
3 tbsp butter, cut into pieces
½ cup freshly grated Parmesan or Cheddar cheese
2 egg yolks
freshly grated nutmeg
1 tbsp toasted bread crumbs

Preheat the oven to moderately hot (190°C/375°F/Gas Mark 5).

Mix the semolina, cornmeal and a little salt together in a mixing bowl. Heat the milk until nearly boiling. Gradually pour on to the dry mixture, stirring well so that it doesn't go lumpy. Transfer the mixture to the saucepan and cook for about 5 minutes, stirring well as the mixture stiffens.

Draw off the heat and stir in the butter pieces, half the grated cheese, the egg yolks, and a generous amount of grated nutmeg. Beat well.

FILLING

350 g/12 oz mushrooms, sliced
1 small onion, peeled and chopped
oil and butter for cooking
1 clove garlic, peeled and chopped
1 tsp chopped fresh thyme
1 tbsp chopped parsley
salt and black pepper

Butter a ring mould or baking dish well, and sprinkle half the breadcrumbs over the surface. Put the polenta mixture in, pressing it down and to the side, and levelling it with a spoon dipped in cold water. Sprinkle the remaining breadcrumbs over and put to bake for 40 minutes, or until it is risen and browned.

To make the filling, soften the onion in a mixture of oil and butter. Add the garlic and then the sliced mushrooms. Cook quickly, adding the thyme and a little parsley.

When the polenta case is cooked, turn it out (or serve straight from the cooking dish). Spoon the mushroom filling into the centre, sprinkle over the remaining parsley and cheese, and serve.

This could be one of the most useful dishes in any cook's repertoire, because it can be served with tomato sauce, or ratatouille for a vegetarian main course, or a meat dish.

Don't forget the nutmeg – an essential ingredient.

FILLING

¾ lb mushrooms, sliced
1 small onion, peeled and chopped
oil and butter for cooking
1 clove garlic, peeled and chopped
1 tsp chopped fresh thyme
1 tbsp chopped parsley
salt and black pepper

BLINIS

A Russian form of yeast pancake, these can be made with all buckwheat flour, or, as here, with half buckwheat and half wheat flour. They are small and plump, with the distinctively buckwheat taste. Traditionally eaten with caviar and soured cream, they are wonderfully versatile — delicious with anything fishy, such as taramasalata, or devilled herring roes, and melted butter or yogurt.

THIS WILL MAKE ABOUT 25

METRIC/IMPERIAL
150 ml/¼ pint milk
150 ml/¼ pint water
1 tsp dried yeast
½ tsp sugar
100 g/4 oz buckwheat flour
100 g/4 oz white flour
½ tsp salt
2 eggs, separated
25 g/1 oz butter, melted
butter or oil for frying

AMERICAN
⅔ cup milk
⅔ cup water
1 tsp active dry yeast
½ tsp sugar
1 cup buckwheat flour
¾ cup white flour
½ tsp salt
2 eggs, separated
2 tbsp butter, melted
butter or oil for frying

Warm the milk and water to blood heat, and mix.

Mix the yeast and sugar together in a small bowl, add a little of the warm liquid, and leave in a warm place for about 10 minutes, until it froths up.

Meanwhile, make a thick batter with the flours, salt, egg yolks, melted butter and remaining milk and water. When the yeast mixture is ready, add to the batter. Cover and leave to rise for 30 minutes.

Beat the egg whites stiffly, and fold in. The batter will be thicker than for an ordinary pancake.

Use a large frying pan, and cook 3 or 4 blinis at once. They should be about 10 cm/4 in diameter. Fry spoonfuls of the batter in butter or oil, turning after about 2 minutes, when holes appear in the top. Pile up and keep warm in a cloth.

SERVING SUGGESTIONS

Pour a little melted butter over. Spread with caviar or lumpfish roe, and top with a spoonful of sour cream.

Serve with creamed haddock and soft-boiled eggs, and pour over sour cream, fromage blanc or crème fraîche.

Serve with bacon for a quick brunch, with Tzatziki (see page 28). Or use any canned fish you have in the store cupboard.

Blinis can also be eaten as a dessert — try them with damson jam and cream.

BAJAN BLACK BEAN SOUP

Arriving stiff and crumpled inside and out after an eleven
hour flight, this was my first taste of Bajan cooking, and I ate
it late at night trying to imagine the sea beyond a dark frieze
of languorous palms. Dense but smooth, with a snap of chilli,
the soup was both homely and exotic, and very restoring.
Barbados produces splendid ham and bacon, and a ham stock
is what makes this different from other Caribbean variants.
Or, as here, use a hock, soaked first to remove some salt.

SERVES 6–8

METRIC/IMPERIAL
450 g/1 lb dried black or turtle beans, soaked overnight
1 large or 2 small bacon hocks
2.75–3.4 litres/5–6 pints water
3 tbsp olive oil
2–3 large onions, peeled and coarsely chopped
4 cloves garlic, peeled and crushed
3 fresh green chillies, or 2 dried red chillies, deseeded, chopped roughly
8 allspice berries, coarsely crushed
grated rind and juice of 1 lemon
2 tsp brown sugar, or 1 tsp molasses
3 tbsp tomato purée
salt
175 ml/6 fl oz crème fraîche or soured cream

Put the drained beans and hock in a very large pan, cover with the cold water and bring gradually to the boil. Leave to simmer while you prepare the other ingredients.

In a frying pan heat the olive oil, then gently fry the onion, garlic and chilli with the allspice and lemon rind, stirring occasionally, till the onions are translucent. Add this mixture to the beans and go on simmering for 2 hours, by which time the beans should be tender. At this point add the sugar, lemon juice, and tomato purée. Cook for another 30 minutes. Add salt if necessary.

Remove the hock, and pick off any meat. If you would like a smooth soup, as mine was, process the mixture in batches and return with the meat to the pan. Otherwise, for a rougher texture crush with a potato masher. If the mixture seems too thick at this stage, add more water and bring back to the boil for a minute or two.

Ladle into bowls, with a spoonful or two of cream stirred in, and serve with crusty bread.

If you are feeling lavish, a couple of spoons of dark rum added towards the end give a Bajan fillip.

AMERICAN
1 lb (about 2½ cups) dried black beans, soaked overnight
1 large or 2 small ham hocks
3–3½ quarts water
3 tbsp olive oil
2–3 large onions, peeled and coarsely chopped
4 cloves garlic, peeled and minced
3 small fresh green chili peppers, or 2 small dried red chili peppers, seeded, chopped roughly
8 allspice berries, coarsely crushed
grated rind and juice of 1 lemon
2 tsp brown sugar, or 1 tsp molasses
3 tbsp tomato paste
salt
¾ cup crème fraîche or sour cream

HUMMUS

Not unlike a vegetarian equivalent of taramasalata, this is a popular dip which most people eat with hot pitta bread as an appetizer. As with tarama, most people season to please themselves. I frequently cheat, using canned chick peas.

METRIC/IMPERIAL
225 g/8 oz cooked chick
  peas, dried or canned
2–3 cloves garlic, peeled
  and crushed
juice of 1–2 lemons
2–3 tbsp fruity olive oil
salt and black pepper
1 tsp ground cumin
1 tbsp tahini (optional)
paprika or cayenne to
  garnish

Drain the chick peas, reserving a little of the liquid. Process with the garlic, some lemon juice and the olive oil till smooth. Season with salt and pepper and cumin. Taste and add more lemon juice if it seems bland. A little reserved thick pea liquid will make a more diluted cream. A spoonful of tahini will make it more nutty and good for you.

Serve spooned out on to a flat, decorative dish, with a pattern of paprika or cayenne on top.

AMERICAN
½ lb (1⅓ cups) cooked
  chick peas, dried or
  canned
2–3 cloves garlic, peeled
  and minced
juice of 1–2 lemons
2–3 tbsp fruity olive oil
salt and black pepper
1 tsp ground cumin
1 tbsp tahini (optional)
paprika or cayenne to
  garnish

THUNDER AND LIGHTNING
(Chick Peas with Pasta)

This seems destined for using up leftover chick peas, or an emergency way of stretching canned peas, but it is worth keeping in mind because the sum is greater than the parts. It can be served as an appetizer or to accompany a meat dish.

METRIC/IMPERIAL
175 g/6 oz cooked chick
  peas, dried or canned
2 tbsp olive oil
2 cloves garlic, peeled and
  finely chopped
225 g/8 oz pasta shapes
  such as farfalle
salt and black pepper
2 tbsp finely chopped fresh
  parsley

Drain the chick peas. Heat the oil in a medium-sized saucepan, add the chick peas and garlic and heat slowly, shaking and turning them once or twice.

Meanwhile, cook the pasta in a large pan of boiling salted water till al dente. Drain and rinse with hot water.

Combine the hot chick peas and hot pasta in a serving dish, salt and pepper generously, and serve sprinkled with the chopped parsley.

A few spoonfuls of suitable pasta sauce (fresh tomato or Bolognese) or some frizzled scraps of bacon can be added to this dish to make it more substantial.

AMERICAN
1 cup cooked chick peas,
  dried or canned
2 tbsp olive oil
2 cloves garlic, peeled and
  finely chopped
½ lb pasta shapes such as
  farfalle
salt and black pepper
2 tbsp finely chopped fresh
  parsley

BAKED BARLEY

I first began experimenting with barley when I couldn't get hold of buckwheat. I discovered then that its nutty taste and chewy texture made an agreeable alternative to rice. It goes well with sausages, gammon rashers or ham slices, or plain bacon and eggs.

SERVES 2

METRIC/IMPERIAL
115 g/4 oz pearl barley
900 ml/1½ pints water
1 stock cube – chicken, beef or vegetable
1 tbsp soy sauce
salt and black pepper
50 g/2 oz butter
1 tbsp grated Cheddar or Parmesan cheese (optional)

Preheat the oven to moderate (180°C/350°F/Gas Mark 4).

Bring the water to the boil with the stock cube. Pour in the barley and cook, covered, till just tender but not mushy – about 30 minutes. Drain, turn into an oven dish and stir in the soy sauce and salt and pepper to taste.

Dot with the butter and sprinkle over the cheese. Bake for 20 minutes.

Leftover barley can be used like cooked rice, and for stuffings.

AMERICAN
heaping ½ cup pearl barley
3¾ cups water
1 bouillon cube – chicken, beef or vegetable
1 tbsp soy sauce
salt and black pepper
4 tbsp butter
1 tbsp grated Cheddar or Parmesan cheese (optioal)

KASHA WITH MUSHROOMS AND SOUR CREAM

A classic Russian dish, this exploits the affinity between earthy buckwheat and fresh or dried fungi. Good with ordinary commercial mushrooms, it is even better if you add a few dried ones like the Italian porcini. Here the kasha is first coated with egg, to enrich it. This is a dish to serve on its own, but it also makes a festive accompaniment to all kinds of meat and game.

METRIC/IMPERIAL
- 225 g/8 oz coarse-grade buckwheat groats (kasha)
- 1 egg, beaten
- 450 ml/¾ pint boiling water
- salt and black pepper
- 100 g/3½ oz butter
- 450 g/1 lb button mushrooms, chopped fairly small, stems and all
- 2 or 3 porcini, soaked in warm water to soften and drained
- 175 ml/6 fl oz soured cream or smetana
- 3 tbsp finely chopped fresh parsley or dill

AMERICAN
- ½ lb (1 heaping cup) coarse-grade buckwheat groats (kasha)
- 1 egg, beaten
- 2 cups boiling water
- salt and black pepper
- 7 tbsp butter
- 1 lb button mushrooms, chopped fairly small, stalks and all
- 2 or 3 porcini, soaked in warm water to soften and drained
- ¾ cup sour cream
- 3 tbsp finely chopped fresh parsley or dill

Preheat the oven to moderate (180°C/350°F/Gas Mark 4).

Mix the buckwheat with the beaten egg, then toast in a dry pan over medium heat to cook out the moisture. Add the boiling water, season with salt and pepper and turn into an oiled oven dish. Dot the top with 50 g/2 oz/4 tbsp butter and bake for 40 minutes.

Meanwhile, gently fry mushrooms and porcini in 25 g/1 oz/2 tbsp butter till dryish and softened. Remove from the heat, stir in the cream and herbs and season.

Mix the mushrooms with the cooked kasha, dot with the remaining butter and bake for 10 minutes or till piping hot.

JOHNNYCAKE

Not just folkloric, but something akin to soda bread made with cornmeal instead of wheat flour. In the American Midwest of which Della Lutes writes so freshly in *The Country Kitchen*, a johnnycake was eaten hot for breakfast, doused in syrup or honey, or fried with bacon and eggs. This is her turn-of-the-century recipe.

METRIC/IMPERIAL
- 450 ml/¾ pint buttermilk
- 3 eggs
- 175 g/6 oz yellow cornmeal
- 1 tsp salt
- 1 tsp bicarbonate of soda
- 1 tbsp hot water
- 25 g/1 oz butter, melted

AMERICAN
- 2 cups buttermilk
- 3 eggs
- 1½ cups yellow cornmeal
- 1 tsp salt
- 1 tsp baking soda
- 1 tsp hot water
- 2 tbsp butter, melted

Preheat the oven to moderate (180°C/350°F/Gas Mark 4). Grease an 18 × 25 cm/7 × 10 inch tin with lard or oil.

Beat the buttermilk and eggs together till pale and light, or process using the pastry blade. Add the cornmeal and salt gradually, processing in short bursts, or beating well. Dissolve the soda in the hot water and add with the butter to the cornmeal batter.

Pour into the prepared tin and bake for 30–40 minutes till crisp.

KHICHRI

A spicy mixture of rice and one of the many varieties of dhal (usually mung in India but I often substitute green lentils), this is held to be the master recipe which Anglo~India modified and added to, to produce the much simpler but also good Kedgeree.

METRIC/IMPERIAL

450 g/1 lb patna or basmati rice
225 g/8 oz mung dhal or green lentils
75 g/3 oz butter or ghee
1 onion, peeled and chopped
2 cloves garlic, peeled and chopped
1 small cube fresh ginger, peeled and grated
½ tsp ground cinnamon
1 tsp turmeric
3 cloves, bruised
3 cardamom pods, bruised
3 fresh chillies, deseeded and sliced (optional)
2.75 litres/5 pints boiling water
salt

Wash and pick over the rice and dhal or lentils, then leave soaking in cold water while you prepare the spicy mixture.

Melt the butter or ghee in a heavy pan, add the onion, garlic, spices and chillies, and cook over gentle heat till the onions are translucent, stirring constantly. At this point, add the drained rice and dhal or lentils and mix well. Continue frying gently, turning the mixture with a wooden spoon, for 2—3 minutes, till the rice and lentils have absorbed the butter and spices.

Pour over the boiling water and stir, then bring back to the boil. Add salt, lower the heat as far as possible, cover the pan tightly and leave to simmer till the khichri is cooked – 20—30 minutes.

Indians serve this hot, as a soothing rest for tired stomachs, first picking out the whole spices. However, like many spicy dishes, it also "eats well", as they used to say, cold or tepid, with a nice chutney for relish.

AMERICAN

2½ cups patna or basmati rice
½ lb (1 heaping cup) mung dhal or green lentils
6 tbsp butter or ghee
1 onion, peeled and chopped
2 cloves garlic, peeled and chopped
1 small cube fresh ginger root, peeled and grated
½ tsp ground cinnamon
1 tsp turmeric
3 cloves, lightly crushed
3 cardamom pods, lightly crushed
3 small fresh chili peppers, seeded and sliced (optional)
6 pints boiling water
salt

STUFFED QUAIL WITH POLENTA

This is as good a way as I know of cooking farmed quail, those tiny, gamey birds which can emerge dry and wizzened if they are not treated respectfully. Note that this is a peasant dish, a frugal feast combining that North Italian staple, polenta or cornmeal mush, and whatever small birds a farmer might bag on his rounds. It is wonderfully savoury, and would make an original main course for a winter dinner party. Timing is not critical; the birds can be moved to the bottom of the oven for another 20 minutes while the polenta browns on top.

METRIC/IMPERIAL
4 quail
225 g/8 oz coarse-ground
   yellow cornmeal (polenta)
900 ml/1 ½ pints water
2 tbsp olive oil
salt and black pepper
4 tbsp freshly grated
   Parmesan cheese
butter
1 small bunch of spring
   onions, chopped
50 g/2 oz green olives,
   stoned and chopped
4 large rashers smoked
   bacon
1 tsp dried oregano
450 ml/¾ pint tomato
   sauce (see page 25)

Bring the water to the boil in a saucepan. Gradually pour on to the cornmeal, stirring well so that it doesn't go lumpy, then pour back into the saucepan. Cook for about 5 minutes, stirring the mush with a wooden spoon, till it begins to come away from the sides of the pan. Add the olive oil, salt and black pepper to taste, and half the Parmesan and mix well. Turn out on to a wet slab or plate and leave to go cold.

An hour before the meal, cut the polenta into squares and arrange them like overlapping tiles in a flat earthenware dish. Dot with butter and sprinkle with the remaining cheese.

Preheat the oven to moderately hot (190°C/375°F/Gas Mark 5). Put the dish of polenta in the bottom of the oven and leave to bake while you prepare the quail.

Wipe the quail inside and out. Mix the spring onions, olives and oregano, and use to stuff the birds. Wrap in bacon, then roast on the top shelf of the oven. After 35—40 minutes, swap the dishes round and cook for another 15—20 minutes.

Serve the quail on top of the polenta slices, which should now be crusty and golden, and pass the hot tomato sauce around separately.

AMERICAN
4 quail
2 cups coarse-ground
   yellow cornmeal (polenta)
3¾ cups water
2 tbsp olive oil
salt and black pepper
4 tbsp freshly grated
   Parmesan cheese
butter
1 small bunch of scallions,
   chopped
⅓ cup green olives, pitted
   and chopped
1 tsp dried oregano
4—8 slices bacon
2 cups tomato sauce (see
   page 25)

CARROT AND WALNUT CAKE

A moist cake, that keeps well. The cinnamon taste may seem a bit strange at first. You *can* fill it with buttercream, or with chestnut purée mixed with butter, but it doesn't really need any embellishment.

METRIC/IMPERIAL
115 g/4 oz carrots, peeled and finely grated
85 g/3 oz butter
115 g/4 oz light muscovado sugar
1 egg, beaten
115 g/4 oz wholemeal flour
pinch of salt
1½ tsp baking powder
1 tsp ground cinnamon
50 g/2 oz shelled walnuts, chopped

Preheat the oven to moderate (180°C/350°/F/Gas Mark 4).

Cream the butter and sugar together, then beat in the egg. Stir in the flour, salt, baking powder and cinnamon. Add the grated carrot and chopped walnuts and stir thoroughly.

Turn into a greased small loaf tin or 18 cm/7 inch round cake tin. Bake for 45 minutes to 1 hour.

AMERICAN
1 cup finely grated carrots
6 tbsp butter
⅔ cup firmly packed light brown sugar
1 egg, beaten
1 cup whole wheat flour
pinch of salt
1½ tsp baking powder
1 tsp ground cinnamon
½ cup chopped walnuts

FRITTELLE DI SAN GIUSEPPE

An Italian friend said these were her favourite food as a child. They are little rounds of lemon-flavoured rice, not too sweet, eaten in Italy at the beginning of Spring, and especially on March 19th, the feast of St Joseph.

METRIC/IMPERIAL
6 tbsp cooked rice
grated rind and juice of 1 lemon
2 tbsp flour
1 egg, lightly beaten
2 tsp sugar
1 tsp vanilla essence
butter for frying

Mix all the ingredients together and form into small balls. Press them flat, and fry them gently, turning once, in a little butter.

Serve plain, or dusted in icing/confectioners' sugar.

AMERICAN
6 tbsp cooked rice
grated rind and juice of 1 lemon
2 tbsp flour
1 egg, lightly beaten
2 tsp sugar
1 tsp vanilla extract
butter for frying

DATE SHORTBREAD

The oats give this sweet and melting mixture a touch of
sourness and a little extra chewiness. Serve as a dessert, with
cream or yogurt, or plain any time of day or night.

METRIC/IMPERIAL
450 g/1 lb dried stoned
    dates
175 /6 oz rolled oats
175 g/6 oz flour
1 tsp bicarbonate of soda
pinch of salt
175 g/6 oz butter or
    margarine

Preheat the oven to moderate (180°C/350°F/Gas
Mark 4).
    Break up the dates roughly, and put them to
soften for a few minutes in a little water.
    Put the oats, flour, soda and salt in a bowl and
rub in the fat. Knead together to make a stiff paste.
    Divide in half and roll out each piece to the same
size; this can be to fit a round sandwich/layer cake
tin or a Swiss/jelly roll tin. Place one piece in the
greased pan and cover with the softened dates.
Place the second layer of paste on top. Bake for
about 40 minutes.
    Serve warm or cold.

AMERICAN
1 lb dried pitted dates
2 cups rolled oats
1⅓ cups flour
1 tsp baking soda
pinch of salt
1½ sticks butter or
    margarine

INTERNATIONAL STYLE

If the global village concept has caught on nowhere else, it has certainly made an astonishing difference to the way we shop, cook and eat. Internationalism in eating starts in the stores, where delicacies unheard of a decade ago, like lemon grass, mangoes and cardamoms, now compete for space on supermarket shelves. It carries through into cooking, where the menu might consist of a scatter of snack dishes drawn from holiday experiences all over the place – Tunisian salad, Greek meze, Thai fish dishes, Scandinavian dips, Japanese tempura. Though there may be moments when the internationalism gets a little out of hand, on the whole its effects have been entirely beneficial. Eclecticism reigns, stimulating our culinary imaginations, broadening our home cooking out of all recognition, and almost certainly improving our health by introducing us to all sorts of delicious high-fibre, low-cholesterol foods cooked in a plainer, cleaner fashion.

BORTSCH

This is a soup which really does need some good stock, preferably beef, although a rich chicken stock will do. You can use the big beetroots which normally take too long to cook as a vegetable.

METRIC/IMPERIAL
25 g/1 oz butter
1 large onion, peeled and chopped
1 clove garlic, peeled and finely chopped
2 large beetroot (about 350 g/12 oz), peeled and grated
2 carrots, peeled and cut into matchsticks
2 large tomatoes, peeled and chopped
1.5 litres/2½ pints beef or chicken stock
1 bay leaf
pinch of caraway seeds
salt and black pepper
a good squeeze of lemon juice
150 ml/¼ pint soured or single cream

In a saucepan, melt the butter, add the onion and garlic and brown gently. Stir in the grated beetroot, carrots and tomatoes and cook a little. Pour on the stock, then add the bay leaf, caraway seeds, and salt and pepper to taste and bring to the boil. Simmer the soup for about 1½ hours.

Fish out the bay leaf. Add a good squeeze of lemon juice, and taste the soup for seasoning. You can either serve the soup with all the vegetables in it, or spoon out some with a slotted spoon, or strain out all the vegetables and return the soup to the pan to reheat.

Serve with the cream poured into each bowlful, the white swirling prettily into the dark red soup.

AMERICAN
2 tbsp butter
1 large onion, peeled and chopped
1 clove garlic, peeled and finely chopped
2 large beetroot (about ¾ lb), peeled and grated
2 carrots, peeled and cut into matchsticks
2 large tomatoes, peeled and chopped
1½ quarts beef or chicken stock
1 bay leaf
pinch of caraway seeds
salt and black pepper
a good squeeze of lemon juice
⅔ cup sour or light cream

BRULE JOL

This was the single most unusual flavour I tasted in Barbados, served up very cold on lettuce leaves. It is curious enough to need describing. Salt fish well soaked is shredded fine and then mixed with onion, hot chillies, lime juice and a little olive oil and left for a day or two in the refrigerator to merge the flavours. It has a rousing, tingling taste which will be a hit with anyone who enjoys seviche.

METRIC/IMPERIAL
225 g/8 oz salt cod
1 onion, peeled and finely
   chopped
2 fresh green chillies,
   deseeded and chopped
juice of 1–2 limes or lemons
1 tbsp olive oil
½ tsp Angostura bitters

Soak the salt cod in cold water for 24 hours, changing the water four times. Drain the fish, remove any bones, skin and dark flesh, and shred or flake it with your fingers. Pat dry with kitchen paper.

Mix in the remaining ingredients and refrigerate in a bowl covered with clingfilm.

This makes a lively appetizer served with toast or crackers and a selection of raw vegetable strips, on lettuce, as I had it, or piled into avocado halves.

AMERICAN
½ lb salt cod
1 onion, peeled and finely
   chopped
2 small fresh green chili
   peppers, seeded and
   chopped
juice of 1–2 limes or lemons
1 tbsp olive oil
½ tsp Angostura bitters

TOMATO SALAD WITH CAERPHILLY OR FETA CHEESE

This is obviously a relation of the Greek salad made with feta cheese, which is not always easy to come by. In any case, Caerphilly is an excellent cheese and not a poor relation.

METRIC/IMPERIAL
450 g/1 lb tomatoes, peeled
   and sliced
1 onion, peeled and thinly
   sliced
50 g/2 oz black olives
about 50–75 g/2–3 oz
   Caerphilly cheese,
   crumbled
vinaigrette dressing
chopped fresh herbs such as
   thyme, basil and
   marjoram

Arrange the tomatoes on a serving plate, spread over the sliced onion and sprinkle over the olives and the crumbled cheese. Pour over a little dressing, made with olive oil if possible, with some chopped fresh herbs added.

AMERICAN
1 lb tomatoes, peeled and
   sliced
1 onion, peeled and thinly
   sliced
⅓ cup black olives
about 2–3 oz crumbly white
   cheese such as Caerphilly
   or feta, crumbled
vinaigrette dressing
chopped fresh herbs such as
   thyme, basil and
   marjoram

TARAMASALATA

There is no definitive recipe for this deliciously pungent fishy paste or cream, which is eaten all around the Mediterranean and in my kitchen every Sunday lunch. Our recipe has this in common with the indigenous ones, that it in no way resembles the nasty pink fluff peddled in delicatessens, and Greek restaurants who should know better. It is strong and garlicky, and we eat it piled on hot toast with other pickled fish and salads. A food processor makes preparation a cinch.

METRIC/IMPERIAL
225 g/8 oz smoked cod's roe in one piece
3 slices decent bread, crusts removed
120 ml/4 fl oz milk
3–4 tbsp olive oil
1 small onion, peeled and coarsely chopped
2–3 cloves garlic, peeled
juice of 1 lemon
plain yogurt
black pepper
pinch of ground cumin
paprika or cayenne to garnish

Put the roe on a board and with a small spoon scrape all the soft roe off the skin. Put the roe into the food processor. Soak the bread in the milk, then lightly squeeze it and crumble into the processor. Blend briefly. Add the olive oil, onion and garlic to the processor and blend till smooth. The taramasalata will be very thick still.

Add the remaining ingredients a little at a time, tasting as you go: lemon juice sharpens the flavour, yogurt smooths and extends the tarama (useful if you suddenly have more people to feed) and pepper and cumin add resonance and bite. Don't overdo the yogurt, however, because the salata should be thick enough to spread on toast or pitta bread without pouring off the sides.

Spoon into a couple of flat bowls, and sprinkle a little paprika or cayenne on top. Serve at room temperature or chilled. It keeps well in the refrigerator.

AMERICAN
½ lb smoked cod's or carp's roe in one piece
3 slices firm-textured bread, crusts removed
½ cup milk
3–4 tbsp olive oil
1 small onion, peeled and coarsely chopped
2–3 cloves garlic, peeled
juice of 1 lemon
plain yogurt
black pepper
pinch of ground cumin
paprika or cayenne to garnish

BAKED LEMON CHICKEN
(Faito Sto Forno)

Artist Polly Hope spends a lot of time in Greece, and likes to cook the straightforward meal-in-a-pan dishes which village women used to send to be cooked in the baker's oven. The essence of such a dish is simplicity, flexibility — like you could substitute slices or chops of pork or lamb — and a good tempered way of being able to take longer cooking without falling to bits. Lots of freshly squeezed lemon juice is the flavouring secret.

SERVES 8–10

METRIC/IMPERIAL
2 × 1.5 kg/3–3½ lb chickens, jointed
salt and black pepper
4 tbsp flour
oil for frying
900 g/2 lb potatoes, peeled and thickly sliced
6 cloves garlic, peeled and chopped
2 tbsp chopped fresh herbs such as tarragon, oregano, thyme or parsley, or 1 tsp dried herbs
450 ml/¾ pint freshly squeezed lemon juice, strained

AMERICAN
2 × 3–3½ lb chickens, cut up
salt and black pepper
4 tbsp flour
oil for frying
2 lb potatoes, peeled and thickly sliced
6 cloves garlic, peeled and chopped
2 tbsp chopped fresh herbs such as tarragon, oregano, thyme or parsley, or 1 tsp dried herbs
2 cups freshly squeezed lemon juice, strained

Preheat the oven to moderate (180°C/350°F/Gas Mark 4).

Wipe the chicken pieces dry with kitchen paper, rub with salt and pepper and coat with flour. Heat oil in a large frying pan and fry the chicken, turning frequently, till golden brown on all sides.

Lay the chicken pieces flat in a roasting pan or shallow ovenproof dish. Fit potato slices in all around, sprinkle over the garlic, herbs, salt and a great deal of black pepper, and pour over the lemon juice. Put to cook in the oven for 1½–2 hours or till the potatoes are tender, the meat golden and the whole thing smells wonderful. If towards the end of the cooking time the dish seems to be drying out too much, turn the heat down a notch and sprinkle over a few tablespoons of water.

Serve with a classic Greek salad of tomatoes, olives, onion and cubes of feta cheese.

CORN FRITTERS

MEXICAN CORN FRITTERS

METRIC/IMPERIAL
225 g/8 oz sweetcorn
   kernels, cooked
50 g/2 oz self-raising flour
2 eggs, lightly beaten
2 tbsp grated cheese
butter and sunflower oil for
   frying

Mix all the ingredients together. Heat enough butter and oil to cover the bottom of a frying pan, until smoking hot. Fry spoonfuls of the corn mixture, turning, until brown on both sides. Serve with Guacamole (page 99) and bacon.

AMERICAN
1 cup cooked corn kernels
heaping ⅓ cup self-rising
   flour
2 eggs, lightly beaten
2 tbsp grated cheese
butter and sunflower oil for
   frying

CORN FRITTERS TWO

This is a slightly bulkier version, very good served instead of dumplings with a beef stew, or to accompany a winter vegetable soup for a quick and nutritious meal.

METRIC/IMPERIAL
125 g/4 oz sweetcorn
   kernels, cooked
50 g/2 oz fresh white
   breadcrumbs
½ tsp baking powder
1 tbsp cream
2 eggs, separated
salt and black pepper
butter and sunflower oil for
   frying

Mix together the corn, breadcrumbs, baking powder, cream, egg yolks and salt and pepper to taste. Beat the egg whites until stiff, and fold in. Fry until brown on both sides.

AMERICAN
½ cup cooked corn kernels
1 cup fresh white
   breadcrumbs
½ tsp baking powder
1 tbsp cream
2 eggs, separated
salt and black pepper
butter and sunflower oil for
   frying

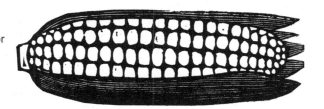

POTATO GNOCCHI WITH CHICKEN LIVER SAUCE

METRIC/IMPERIAL
900 g/2 lb potatoes, peeled
225 g/8 oz flour
2 eggs
freshly grated nutmeg
salt and black pepper
freshly grated Parmesan or
    Cheddar cheese
butter

SAUCE
1 small onion, peeled and
    chopped
25 g/1 oz butter
2 tbsp olive oil
225 g/8 oz chicken livers,
    chopped
450 g/1 lb tomatoes, peeled
    and chopped, or 400-g/
    14-oz can tomatoes
1 bay leaf

AMERICAN
2 lb potatoes, peeled
1¾ cups flour
2 eggs
freshly grated nutmeg
salt and black pepper
freshly grated Parmesan or
    Cheddar cheese
butter

SAUCE
1 small onion, peeled and
    chopped
2 tbsp butter
2 tbsp olive oil
½ lb chicken livers, chopped
1 lb tomatoes, peeled and
    chopped, or 14-oz can
    tomatoes
1 bay leaf

Boil the potatoes, drain and return to the pan to dry out over low heat. Put through a mouli or potato ricer, or mash. Add the flour, eggs, a little nutmeg and salt and pepper to taste. Mix to a dough, then form into a long roll on a floured board. Cut into little pieces, about 2.5 cm/1 in square. Roll each piece over a fork to curve it, or press against the wrong side of a grater to make a pattern.

Prepare the sauce by frying the onion in the butter and oil. Add the chicken livers and fry until they are brown. Add the tomatoes, bay leaf, and salt and pepper to taste. Let the sauce simmer while the gnocchi are cooking.

Sprinkle cheese in a serving dish and put to keep warm. Bring a large pan of salted water to the boil and drop in some gnocchi, allowing them plenty of space. As soon as they rise to the surface, remove them with a slotted spoon and put them in the hot dish. Sprinkle them with cheese, dot with butter and keep hot. Repeat with the remaining gnocchi.

Serve with the chicken liver sauce.

These gnocchi are also very good baked in a hot oven (225°C/425°F/Gas Mark 7) for 20–30 minutes. Make the dough into little flattish cakes and put a spot of butter on each one.

Gnocchi can be served alone, with just the butter and cheese, or with a tomato sauce.

TAHINI DIP

Serve with hot pitta bread, tortilla chips or crudités.

METRIC/IMPERIAL
150 ml/¼ pint tahini
   (sesame seed paste)
juice of 2 lemons
2 cloves garlic, peeled and
   crushed
½ tsp salt
½ tsp chilli powder
1 tsp ground cumin
300 ml/½ pint milk
1 tbsp chopped fresh parsley

Mix together the tahini, lemon juice, garlic, salt,
chilli and cumin. Gradually stir or blend in the milk.
Mix in the parsley.

AMERICAN
⅔ cup tahini (sesame seed
   paste)
juice of 2 lemons
2 cloves garlic, peeled and
   minced
½ tsp salt
½ tsp chili powder
1 tsp ground cumin
1¼ cups milk
1 tbsp chopped fresh parsley

JOE'S TANDOORI RABBIT

Joe Tibbets, whose right hand writes plays while his left nurses small businesses into prosperous life, has a fund of low cost recipes with style. This is one he makes using "any rabbit pieces, especially frozen ones", and his friends assume it is the tenderest chicken.

METRIC/IMPERIAL
675–900 g/1½–2 lb rabbit, jointed
1 tsp cumin seeds
1 tsp grated fresh ginger
2 cloves garlic, peeled and finely chopped
seeds from 4 cardamom pods
1 tsp paprika or tandoori paste
juice of ½ lemon
1 red chilli, deseeded (optional)
tiny pinch of salt
150 ml/¼ pint plain yogurt
melted ghee or butter

AMERICAN
1½–2 lb rabbit, cut up
1 tsp cumin seeds
1 tsp grated fresh ginger root
2 cloves garlic, peeled and finely chopped
seeds from 4 cardamom pods
1 tsp paprika or tandoori paste
juice of ½ lemon
1 small chili pepper, deseeded (optional)
tiny pinch of salt
⅔ cup plain yogurt
melted ghee or butter

Put the cumin seeds in a dry pan over a low flame and toast till the aniseed smell rises. Tip into a food processor and add the ginger, garlic, cardamom seeds, paprika, lemon juice, chilli, salt and yogurt and blend to a smooth paste. Prick the rabbit pieces well all over, pour over the marinade and turn to coat well. Leave overnight in the refrigerator or if pressed, for a few hours at room temperature.

To cook, remove the pieces from the refrigerator and leave to come to room temperature for an hour or so.

Preheat the grill/broiler or preheat the oven to very hot (240°C/475°F/Gas Mark 9).

Remove the rabbit from the marinade and brush with melted ghee or butter. Cook for 15–20 minutes on a wire rack under the grill/broiler, or for 20–30 minutes in the oven, turning from time to time and brushing or basting with more melted ghee.

Serve with pilao rice, and a chunky Indian-style salad of cucumber, onion and tomato dressed with lemon juice, oil and chopped fresh coriander.

PASTA WITH MEATBALLS
AND TOMATO SAUCE

This is a splendid rich dish, which will feed 4 ravenous people, or 6 polite ones, depending on the amount of spaghetti or other pasta you serve with it. Allow at least 100 g/4 oz pasta per person for a one-dish meal. Serve with grated cheese and a green salad. It will make about 20 meatballs.

METRIC/IMPERIAL

450 g/1 lb minced beef
2 slices pork or a little bacon, minced
3 slices bread, moistened with 3 tbsp milk
50 g/2 oz Parmesan or Cheddar cheese, freshly grated
1 clove garlic, peeled and chopped
½ onion, peeled and grated
1 tbsp chopped parsley
1 tsp chopped fresh thyme
1 tsp chopped fresh marjoram
salt and black pepper
1 egg, beaten
flour for coating
olive oil or butter for frying
tomato spaghetti sauce (see page 25)
about 450 g/1 lb pasta

Mix together the beef, pork, bread, cheese, garlic, onion, herbs, seasoning and egg in a mixing bowl with your hands, which is messy but efficient. Keep your hands damp. Now wash all the bits off your hands, rinse them under the cold tap, take a spoonful of the mixture and form it into a ball. There'll be no problem with stickiness. Lightly flour the meatballs, and brown well in a little olive oil or butter.

Drop the meatballs into the tomato sauce, and simmer for about 30 minutes.

While this is happening, cook the pasta in lots of boiling water. Drain the pasta, and serve topped with the meatballs and sauce.

AMERICAN

1 lb ground beef
2 slices pork or a little bacon, ground
3 slices bread, moistened with 3 tbsp milk
½ cup freshly grated Parmesan or Cheddar cheese
1 clove garlic, peeled and chopped
½ onion, peeled and grated
1 tbsp chopped parsley
1 tsp chopped fresh thyme
1 tsp chopped fresh marjoram
salt and black pepper
1 egg, beaten
flour for coating
olive oil or butter for frying
tomato spaghetti sauce (see page 25)
about 1 lb pasta

CHICKEN TIKKA

A delicious hot and spicy way of cooking chicken, this can either be done as a kebab, with breast meat of chicken, or with whole chicken legs.

METRIC/IMPERIAL
4 chicken breasts, skinned and boned, or chicken legs
150 ml/¼ pint Greek-style strained yogurt
4 cloves garlic, peeled and crushed
4 cm/1½ in cube fresh ginger, peeled and chopped
1 small onion, peeled and grated
1 tsp chilli powder
1 tbsp ground coriander

Mix together all the ingredients except the chicken. If using chicken breasts, cut them into roughly 2.5 cm/1 in cubes. If you are using chicken legs, score the flesh. Leave the chicken in the yogurt mixture overnight, if possible.

To cook the chicken breasts: put them on skewers, coat well with the yogurt mixture and grill/broil for about 8 minutes, turning them at intervals. To cook the chicken legs: lay them on the grill/broiler and cook, turning, for about 10–12 minutes, depending on size.

AMERICAN
4 chicken breast halves, skinned and boned, or chicken legs
⅔ cup thick plain yogurt
4 cloves garlic, peeled and minced
1½ in cube fresh ginger root, peeled and chopped
1 small onion, peeled and grated
1 tsp chili powder
1 tsp ground coriander

STIR-FRIED PORK SLICES

METRIC/IMPERIAL
225 g/8 oz lean boneless pork (fillet or leg), thinly sliced
2 egg whites
1 tbsp cornflour
5 cm/2 in cube fresh ginger, peeled and finely chopped
1 tbsp dry sherry
120 ml/4 fl oz stock or water
salt
3 tbsp sunflower oil
50 g/2 oz canned bamboo shoots, sliced
50 g/2 oz spring onions, cut into strips

Mix the pork with the egg whites and cornflour. Mix together the ginger, sherry, stock and a little salt.

Heat the oil in a wok or large frying pan, drop in the coated pork slices and stir-fry. Remove, and stir-fry the bamboo shoots and spring onions. Return the pork to the pan, add the stock mixture, and heat thoroughly.

Serve on a hot serving dish, with soy sauce.

AMERICAN
½ lb lean boneless pork (tenderloin or leg), thinly sliced
2 egg whites
1 tbsp cornstarch
2 in cube fresh ginger root, peeled and finely chopped
1 tbsp dry sherry
½ cup stock or water
salt
3 tbs sunflower oil
¼ cup sliced canned bamboo shoots
½ cup scallions, cut into strips

GUACAMOLE

Guacamole and tortilla chips, or *totopos*, go together like cheese and pickles. Tortilla chips are available everywhere, as is fresh coriander, which is what gives subtle pungency to a classic guacamole. For speed, use a food processor, but for authenticity, chop the vegetables by hand, and merely *mash* the avocado flesh with a fork, to a roughish pulp.

METRIC/IMPERIAL
2 medium-sized ripe avocados
2 ripe tomatoes, chopped to a pulp
1 onion, peeled and finely chopped
1–3 fresh green chillies, deseeded and finely chopped
salt and black pepper
juice of 1 lime or ½ lemon
1 tbsp finely chopped fresh coriander

Mix the chopped tomatoes, onion and chillies together with salt and pepper to taste, and let stand for an hour or two.

Shortly before serving, halve the avocados, remove stones, scoop out the flesh and mash to a pulp with a fork (or process), sprinkling with the lime or lemon juice. Mix well with the other ingredients and coriander, decorate with a sprig of coriander and serve before the green colour begins to darken.

AMERICAN
2 medium-sized ripe avocados
2 ripe tomatoes, chopped to a pulp
1 onion, peeled and finely chopped
2–3 small fresh green chili peppers, seeded and finely chopped
salt and black pepper
juice of 1 lime or ½ lemon
1 tbsp finely chopped fresh coriander (cilantro)

RABBIT BRAISED WITH GREEN OLIVES AND CAPERS

Rabbit, especially frozen rabbit pieces, can be dry and tough. This Spanish recipe, where the meat is braised slowly in a lemon and oil mixture, counteracts this tendency. Frozen pieces should be well thawed.

METRIC/IMPERIAL
675 g/1½ lb rabbit, jointed, or rabbit pieces
120 ml/4 fl oz lemon juice
120 ml/4 fl oz olive oil
225 ml/8 fl oz water
2 large onions, peeled and sliced
2 cloves garlic, peeled and chopped
salt and black pepper
25 g/1 oz green olives, stoned
1 tbsp capers

Preheat the oven to moderate (180°C/350°F/Gas Mark 4).

Put the rabbit pieces in a flameproof casserole with the lemon juice, oil, water, onion, garlic and seasoning. Cover and bring to the boil on top of the stove.

Process or pound the olives and capers to a paste and add to the casserole shaking to distribute evenly. Transfer the covered pot to the oven and cook for 1½ hours.

Serve with bread and a leafy salad, with fresh herbs in the dressing.

AMERICAN
1½ lb rabbit, cut up, or rabbit pieces
½ cup lemon juice
½ cup olive oil
1 cup water
2 large onions, peeled and sliced
2 cloves garlic, peeled and chopped
salt and black pepper
1 oz large green olives (5–6), pitted
1 tbsp capers

PERUVIAN PEANUT SAUCE WITH POTATOES

METRIC/IMPERIAL
900 g/2 lb potatoes
1 small onion, peeled and chopped
1 small fresh green chilli, finely chopped
6 tbsp sunflower oil
50 g/2 oz shelled peanuts, ground
150 ml/¼ pint milk
50 g/2 oz Cheddar cheese, grated
salt and black pepper

Cook the potatoes in boiling salted water. When tender, drain and peel.

Meanwhile, soften the onion and chilli in the oil. Add the peanuts, milk, cheese, and salt and pepper to taste and simmer until the sauce is thick. It can be blended until smooth in a blender or food processor, or left as it is.

Pour the sauce over the hot cooked potatoes, and serve with hard-boiled eggs and salad.

AMERICAN
2 lb potatoes
1 small onion, peeled and chopped
1 small fresh green chili pepper, finely chopped
6 tbsp sunflower oil
⅓ cup shelled peanuts, ground
⅔ cup milk
½ cup grated Cheddar cheese
salt and black pepper

SQUID WITH CHINESE NOODLES

METRIC/IMPERIAL
350 g/12 oz baby squid
1 onion, peeled and
    chopped
2 tbsp olive oil
25 g/1 oz butter
450 g/1 lb tomatoes, peeled
    and chopped
2 tsp dried dill
4 tbsp red wine
salt and black pepper
350 g/12 oz firm white fish
    fillet (huss is good), diced
350 g/12 oz Chinese thread
    noodles or vermicelli

Baby squid are very tender and not difficult to prepare. Remove the heads from the squid by putting the back of the knife down on them and pulling them out. Cut off the tentacles, and discard the rest. Remove the backbone. Press the back of the knife along the squid, squeezing out the innards, and discard them. Gently scrape off the skin with a sharp knife. You are now left with a white oval-shaped sac. Slice it across to form 5 mm/¼ in rings.

Soften the chopped onion in the oil and butter. Add the squid stirring it as it cooks and becomes opaque. Add the tomatoes, dill, wine and salt and pepper to taste. Cover and simmer for 15 minutes. Now add the white fish fillet, and simmer for another 15 minutes.

Meanwhile, cook the noodles in plenty of boiling salted water for 5 minutes. Drain.

Check the fish mixture for seasoning, and if the sauce has cooked too dry, add a little water. Serve on a hot dish, with the fish and tomato sauce poured over the noodles and well mixed.

 Half quantities will make a good first course.

 Add about 300 ml/½ pint/1¼ cups of mussels or clams and a few prawns/shrimp as decorations if liked.

AMERICAN
¾ lb baby squid
1 onion, peeled and
    chopped
2 tbsp olive oil
2 tbsp butter
1 lb tomatoes, peeled and
    chopped
2 tsp dried dill
4 tbsp red wine
salt and black pepper
¾ lb firm white fish fillet,
    diced
¾ lb Chinese beanthread
    (cellophane) noodles or
    vermicelli

SPICED BEAN CURD

METRIC/IMPERIAL
100 g/4 oz firm bean curd (tofu), cut into cubes
sunflower oil for frying
100 g/4 oz lean boneless beef, minced
100 g/4 oz shelled broad beans
chilli powder to taste
300 ml/½ pint warm water
50 g/2 oz spring onion tops, chopped
1 heaped tsp cornflour
soy sauce to taste

AMERICAN
¼ lb firm bean curd (tofu), cut into cubes
sunflower oil for frying
¼ lb lean boneless beef, ground
¼ lb shelled fava or lima beans
chili powder to taste
1¼ cups warm water
½ cup chopped green scallion tops
1 heaping tsp cornstarch
soy sauce to taste

Heat a wok or heavy frying pan, and pour in a little oil. Heat and then add in order, stir-frying, the beef, the beans and the chilli powder. Pour in the warm water and add the bean curd. Stir gently. Bring to the boil, then reduce the heat and simmer for 15 minutes.

Add the spring onion tops. Turn up the heat, and stir in the cornflour, dissolved in a little cold water. Stir till the sauce thickens.

Serve with plain boiled rice, Chinese/Nappa cabbage, roasted peanuts, and a little bowl of soy sauce.

The Chinese would use garlic tops for this recipe, instead of spring onions. Use chives if you have them. The tops of onions that have bolted would do well too.

STIR-FRIED MUSHROOMS IN OYSTER SAUCE

This will serve 4 with other dishes, such as stir-fry pork slices, noodles and a salad.

METRIC/IMPERIAL
450 g/1 lb button mushrooms
2 tsp cornflour
2 tbsp water
1 tbsp soy sauce
1 tbsp dry sherry
3 tbsp sunflower oil
2 tbsp oyster sauce (Hao Yu)
chopped parsley

AMERICAN
1 lb button mushrooms
2 tsp cornstarch
2 tbsp water
1 tbsp soy sauce
1 tbsp dry sherry
3 tbsp sunflower oil
2 tbsp oyster sauce (Hao Yu)
chopped parsley

Use either a wok or a frying pan.

Mix together the cornflour, water, soy sauce and sherry. Stir-fry the mushrooms in the oil for a couple of minutes. Add the oyster sauce and stir again. Now add the cornflour mixture. As soon as it thickens, give a good stir around, and then transfer to a serving dish and sprinkle parsley over.

POTATOES WITH CORIANDER SAUCE

METRIC/IMPERIAL
450 g/1 lb potatoes
chopped fresh coriander
1 tsp coriander seeds,
  crushed
150 ml/¼ pint fromage
  blanc

Cook the potatoes in boiling salted water; drain and peel.

Mix the coriander and coriander seeds with the cheese and pour over the hot potatoes just before serving.

Single/light cream with a little lemon juice can be used instead of the cheese.

AMERICAN
1 lb potatoes
chopped fresh coriander
  (cilantro)
1 tsp coriander seeds,
  crushed
⅔ cup ricotta or other
  similar smooth white
  cheese, or sour cream

TORRIJAS

A useful quick dessert or snack.

METRIC/IMPERIAL
4 large slices bread
150 ml/¼ pint milk
1 egg, beaten
25 g/1 oz butter
50 g/2 oz clear honey
4 tbsp medium sherry

Preheat the oven to moderate (180°C/350°F/Gas Mark 4).

Remove crusts from the bread unless they are very soft. Cut each slice into three or four strips. Soak in the milk for about 4–5 minutes, then dip the bread in the lightly beaten egg. Fry gently in the butter until light brown.

Place in a casserole or oven dish. Mix the honey and sherry and pour over. Bake for about 30 minutes, until golden and crisp.

Serve piled up on a dish, and eat with a fork or fingers.

AMERICAN
4 large slices bread
⅔ cup milk
1 egg, beaten
2 tbsp butter
2 heaping tbsp clear honey
4 tbsp medium sherry

SYDNEY FRUIT CAKE

This cake earns a place for two reasons — it's a good fruit
cake, and it's the easiest possible cake to make.

METRIC/IMPERIAL
225 g/8 oz self-raising flour
115 g/4 oz sugar
350 g/12 oz mixed dried
 fruit
2 eggs, beaten
115 g/4 oz butter or
 margarine, melted
¼ tsp grated nutmeg
¼ tsp mixed spice
¼ tsp ground cinnamon
120 ml/4 fl oz milk

Preheat the oven to moderate (160°C/325°F/Gas
Mark 3).
 Put all the ingredients into a bowl and beat by
hand for 4—5 minutes or with a beater for a couple
of minutes.
 Turn into a greased and floured 15 cm/6 in cake
tin and bake for 2 hours. Cool in the tin.

AMERICAN
1⅔ cups self-rising flour
½ cup sugar
2 heaping cups mixed dried
 fruit
2 eggs, beaten
1 stick butter or margarine,
 melted
¼ tsp grated nutmeg
¼ tsp apple pie spice
¼ tsp ground cinnamon
½ cup milk

IN GRANDMOTHER'S FOOTSTEPS

Traditional recipes have an honourable place in any cookbook concerned with domestic cookery. Anyone who cooks regularly needs the fun and challenge of novelty: experimentation keeps the creative as well as gastric juices flowing. It's equally true, though, that after a bout of excited innovation in the kitchen, one returns with a sense of relief and homecoming to the tastes and methods one grew up with. What defines traditional cookery, for me, is its rootedness in the land where it evolved. At its best it both distils and consummates the sharply individual flavours, and much polished usages, of a particular region and its produce and people. To palates glutted with choice, the whole world's fruits on display in every supermarket, sampling an apple tart made with fruit from the orchard across the road is a recovery of innocence, one of the rare moments where poor clogged tastebuds bounce up renewed.

TOMATO ICE CREAM

This is very easy to prepare and makes an exotic appetizer for a party. As the cream makes it rich, a little goes a long way.

SERVES 6–8

METRIC/IMPERIAL
225 g/8 oz fresh ripe tomatoes, peeled and chopped
juice of ½ lemon
salt and black pepper
120 ml/4 fl oz whipping cream, whipped

AMERICAN
½ lb fresh ripe tomatoes, peeled and chopped
juice of ½ lemon
salt and black pepper
½ cup heavy cream, whipped

Mash the tomatoes to a pulp. Mix in the juice of the lemon and plenty of black pepper. Fold in the cream and add salt to taste.

Spoon into an ice-tray, and put to freeze. This will probably only take about an hour, because the ice cream is best not entirely frozen. It is ready when it will keep shape sufficiently to turn out of the ice-tray, but is still creamy and soft inside.

Serve on its own, or with a green salad, or as the centre to a sliced tomato salad with vinaigrette dressing.

RAMEKINS OF SALMON WITH GINGER

A delicate dish for an appetizer.

METRIC/IMPERIAL
200-g/7-oz can salmon, drained and flaked
1 tsp grated onion
2 eggs
1 egg yolk
300 ml/½ pint milk
salt and black pepper
4 cm/1½ in cube fresh ginger, peeled and grated
4 tbsp single cream
1 tsp chopped fresh dill

AMERICAN
7-oz can salmon, drained and flaked
1 tsp grated onion
2 eggs
1 egg yolk
1¼ cups milk
salt and black pepper
1½ in cube fresh ginger root, peeled and grated
4 tbsp light cream
1 tsp chopped fresh dill

Preheat the oven to moderate (350°F/180°C/Gas Mark 4).

Mix the salmon with the grated onion. Put a quarter in each ramekin. Beat the eggs and yolk together. Heat the milk, and pour on to the eggs. Season to taste with salt and pepper, and stir in the ginger. Pour the custard over the salmon, and put the ramekins into a baking dish containing about 2.5 cm/1 in of water.

Bake for about 30 minutes, or until the salmon custards are set. Cool completely. Spread a thin layer of dill-flavoured thin cream over the top of each ramekin before serving.

KEDGEREE

The name kedgeree comes from the Hindi, meaning a dish of rice and sesame, and first came into the English language way back in 1625. In early days it was made with lentils as well as rice, and well spiced.

This is the traditional English recipe, which is hard to improve on, basically rice and smoked haddock, but with the option of spicing it up with sesame and curry. This is a generous amount for 4 people as a main dish.

METRIC/IMPERIAL
450 g/1 lb smoked haddock fillet
a little milk and water
350 g/12 oz long-grain rice
225 g/8 oz onions, peeled and chopped
1 tsp curry powder (optional)
75 g/3 oz butter
1 tbsp dark sesame oil (optional)
3 hard-boiled eggs, shelled and chopped
salt and black pepper
1–2 tbsp sesame seeds, toasted (optional)

Put the haddock to simmer in a pan on the stove, or in a moderate oven (180°C/350°F/Gas mark 4), with a little milk and water for 15–20 minutes or until the flesh comes off the bones easily. Drain, and remove all bones and skin. Put in a heated dish to keep warm.

While the fish is cooking, cook the rice in boiling salted water for about 12 minutes. Drain the rice and add to the fish.

Gently fry the chopped onion and curry powder (if used) in half of the butter and the sesame oil until soft. Mix the chopped eggs, onion, fish and rice well together, seasoning with salt and pepper, and adding the remaining butter. The kedgeree should be moist and buttery. Sprinkle over the sesame seeds and serve.

AMERICAN
1 lb smoked haddock fillet (finnan haddie)
a little milk and water
2 cups long-grain rice
½ lb onions, peeled and chopped
1 tsp curry powder (optional)
6 tbsp butter
1 tbsp dark sesame oil (optional)
3 hard-boiled eggs, shelled and chopped
salt and black pepper
1–2 tbsp sesame seeds, toasted (optional)

RABBIT IN ONION SAUCE

It's one of those paradoxes that imported rabbit which has travelled here all the way from China is cheaper than an English rabbit. They look very unappetizing, dark and bloody, but when cooked the flesh is tasty (quite strong) and pale pink in colour. Native rabbits are paler, the flesh almost white when cooked (like chicken), the taste definite but not over strong — but certainly with much more character than any frozen chicken. Soak imported rabbit for several hours in cold water with 1 tablespoon of vinegar to blanch the meat.

METRIC/IMPERIAL
1 rabbit, jointed
1 tbsp vinegar
1 onion, peeled and
    quartered
1 carrot, peeled and sliced
1 bay leaf
thyme
600 ml/1 pint mixed milk
    and water
1 large onion, peeled and
    chopped
25 g/1 oz butter
25 g/1 oz flour
salt and black pepper
100 g/4 oz streaky bacon
    rashers
chopped parsley

AMERICAN
1 rabbit, cut up
1 tbsp vinegar
1 onion, peeled and
    quartered
1 carrot, peeled and sliced
1 bay leaf
thyme
2½ cups mixed milk and
    water
1 large onion, peeled and
    chopped
2 tbsp butter
2 tbsp flour
salt and black pepper
¼ lb thick bacon slices
chopped parsley

Wash the rabbit pieces in cold water with the vinegar in it. Put in a heavy saucepan with the quartered onion, carrot, bay leaf, thyme, milk and water. Simmer till tender – about 1½ hours – and the meat falls easily off the bone.

Take out the rabbit and carefully remove all bones. Put the meat to keep warm in a casserole, if you are making the dish to be eaten right away. (Otherwise the whole dish can be made in advance and gently reheated.) Strain the rabbit stock.

Make the onion sauce by simmering the chopped onion in a little of the rabbit stock until tender; drain. Then make a white sauce with the butter, flour and about 300 ml/½ pint/1¼ cups of rabbit stock. Add the onion and salt and pepper to taste. Pour over the rabbit and keep hot in the oven.

Cut each slice of bacon in half crossways, stretch with the back of the knife and roll up. Grill/broil, turning once, until crisp.

Garnish the rabbit with a little chopped parsley and the bacon rolls. Serve with boiled potatoes and green beans, and redcurrant jelly.

✎ To make a party dish of this, cook little balls of puff pastry to accompany the rabbit, or cover the rabbit with a pastry top.

CHINA CHILO

Not all old English dishes are hearty and rumbustious. This one, collected by Dorothy Hartley in her *Food in England*, is ladylike, a fresh-tasting composition of summery vegetables and lamb. She specifies mutton, which is leaner and tastier than lamb, and obtainable nowadays from halal butchers. It makes a pleasant change from the much spiced and seasoned ragouts currently fashionable — a dish the Cranford ladies might have prepared for each other, "with a flavour of white muslin and spinets".

METRIC/IMPERIAL
50 g/2 oz butter
450 g/1 lb lean boneless lamb or mutton, minced or finely chopped
2–3 lettuces (Cos or butterheart), shredded
350 g/12 oz peas, preferably shelled fresh
bunch of spring onions, roughly chopped
4 tbsp water
½ cucumber, peeled, deseeded and diced
100 g/4 oz mushrooms, sliced
salt and black pepper

Melt the butter in a wide pan over moderate heat, add the meat and turn it till lightly browned, breaking up lumps with a fork. Add the lettuce, fresh peas and onions, and cook for a few moments longer, turning to get them buttery. When it is all hot, and the lettuce limp, add the water. Cover and cook over the lowest heat for 1 hour.

Now add the cucumber, mushrooms, and frozen peas if used. Cover again and cook a further 30 minutes.

Remove the lid, season with salt and pepper, and cook gently for another 10–15 minutes to reduce some of the liquid.

Serve with plain boiled Patna rice, dried off in a low oven, and small young carrots, finished by turning in a little melted butter and a pinch of sugar.

AMERICAN
4 tbsp butter
1 lb lean boneless lamb, ground or finely chopped
2–3 heads lettuce (romaine or butterhead), shredded
2½ cups peas, preferably shelled fresh
bunch of scallions, roughly chopped
4 tbsp water
1 small cucumber, peeled, deseeded and diced
¼ lb mushrooms, sliced
salt and black pepper

SALMAGUNDI

An ancient dish, dating from the 17th century, this comes in several disguises. One version calls it a "sort of vegetable mosaic", while another describes it as basically a mixture of chopped meat, anchovies, boiled eggs and onion. Like the Swedish "eye" dishes, the emphasis is on contrasts of colours and flavours.

METRIC/IMPERIAL ESSENTIAL INGREDIENTS

cooked chicken or other
  white meat, diced
cooked rare beef or ham,
  diced
hard-boiled eggs,
  separated, and whites
  and yolks chopped
anchovy fillets, halved
  lengthways and coiled
smoked mackerel fillet,
  flaked
thinly sliced white and
  purple onion
thinly sliced red cabbage
vinaigrette dressing

EXTRA VEGETABLES

cooked spiced red cabbage
cucumber rings, with
  cooked peas or asparagus
tomatoes
red peppers
cooked broad and runner
  beans in season
radishes and mooli
fresh herbs such as parsley
  and tarragon

If you have not got a huge platter to spread everything out on, arrange separate dishes with a mixture of some of the fish and meat, and one or two vegetables. The meat should be put in little piles. Small piles of chopped egg white and yolk should be arranged among the vegetables. (Old English cooking was very sensitive to colour, especially contrasts of red and white in puddings, with use of gold leaf for decoration, and many sophisticated mixtures.) Pour over a vinaigrette dressing.

AMERICAN ESSENTIAL INGREDIENTS

cooked chicken or other
  white meat, diced
cooked rare beef or ham,
  diced
hard-boiled eggs,
  separated, and whites
  and yolks chopped
anchovy fillets, halved
  lengthwise and coiled
smoked mackerel fillet,
  flaked
thinly sliced white and red
  onion
thinly sliced red cabbage
vinaigrette dressing

EXTRA VEGETABLES

cooked spiced red cabbage
cucumber rings, with
  cooked peas or asparagus
tomatoes
sweet red peppers
cooked fava or lima and
  green beans in season
radishes and daikon
fresh herbs such as parsley
  and tarragon

CHOPS BAKED WITH FENNEL AND POTATOES

Those bulbous Florentine fennel roots are delicious used in salads, but their pungent anise flavour comes across particularly well when they are cooked, and balances the richness of pork or lamb chops. This is one of those dishes which are forgiving about timing. It can be left to look after itself, and won't come to any harm if cooked half an hour longer, at a lower setting.

METRIC/IMPERIAL
4 large pork or 8 lamb chops
1 tbsp cooking oil
4 medium potatoes
2 fennel roots
150 ml/¼ pint white wine, cider or apple juice
salt and black pepper

AMERICAN
4 large pork or 8 lamb chops
1 tbsp cooking oil
4 medium potatoes
2 fennel bulbs
⅔ cup white wine, hard cider or apple juice
salt and black pepper

Preheat the oven to moderate (180°C/350°F/Gas Mark 4).

Heat the oil in a frying pan and sear the chops on both sides. Meanwhile, drop the potatoes into boiling water and part-cook for about 8 minutes; drain. Peel and slice thickly. Cut the feathery green tops off the fennel, reserve, and slice each root into four.

Lay the chops in a large shallow oven-proof dish, with sliced potato and fennel in between. Splash over the wine and sprinkle on a little salt, a lot of pepper and the chopped fennel tops. Cover with a lid, or foil well folded around, and cook in the oven for 1½ hours. (If you want to leave them to cook longer, turn the oven down to the next setting.)

Serve from the same dish, with braised red cabbage or green beans.

CORNISH PASTIES

MAKES 4

METRIC/IMPERIAL
225 g/8 oz minced beef or lamb
1 medium potato, peeled and chopped
1 small onion, peeled and chopped
pinch of dried thyme
pinch of ground mace
½ tsp salt
black pepper
Worcestershire sauce to taste
shortcrust pastry made with 225 g/8 oz flour
beaten egg or milk to glaze

Preheat the oven to hot (220°C/425°F/Gas Mark 7).

Mix all the ingredients for the filling together.

Roll out the pastry, and cut out rounds about 15 cm/6 in diameter (use a small plate or saucer as a guide). Put a quarter of the filling in the centre of each round. Dampen the edges and bring together in the middle, pressing firmly together. Press them into a wavy pattern. Brush over with beaten egg or milk.

Put on a baking sheet and bake for about 30 minutes.

AMERICAN
½ lb ground beef or lamb
1 medium potato, peeled and chopped
1 small onion, peeled and chopped
pinch of dried thyme
pinch of ground mace
½ tsp salt
black pepper
Worcestershire sauce to taste
pie pastry made with 1¾ cups flour
beaten egg or milk to glaze

SAVOURY SARDINE ROLL

This is a piquant, powerful-tasting roll, and a slice or two makes an excellent appetizer.

METRIC/IMPERIAL
225 g/8 oz puff pastry, thawed if frozen
2 tsp French mustard
2 tsp soy sauce
1 clove garlic, peeled and finely chopped
¼ tsp ground ginger, or a little grated fresh ginger
small can sardines in olive oil
1 sharp apple, peeled, cored and finely chopped
1 egg yolk, beaten

Preheat the oven to hot (230°C/450°F/Gas Mark 8).

Roll out the puff pastry thinly, to a long rectangle. Mix the mustard, soy sauce, garlic and ginger well together, and spread over the pastry, leaving the edge free. Mash the sardines and spread them on top. Cover with the apple.

Roll up the pastry, not too tightly, to a long roll, moistening the long edge with water and pressing it together to seal. Join the ends together with a little water. Glaze with beaten egg yolk.

Put on a baking sheet, join downwards. Bake until the pastry is well risen and brown.

AMERICAN
½ lb puff pastry, thawed if frozen
2 tsp Dijon-style mustard
2 tsp soy sauce
1 clove garlic, peeled and finely chopped
¼ tsp ground ginger, or a little grated fresh ginger root
small can sardines in olive oil
1 tart apple, peeled, cored and finely chopped
1 egg yolk, beaten

RAISED PIES WITH GAME
OR MEAT FILLINGS

A homemade raised pie, its sturdy crust housing a medley of meats moistened with well-flavoured stock, is a truly noble offering with only a nominal resemblance to the commercial pork pie, with its pellet of flavourless filling in a cardboardy case. Hot water crust, like suet crust, is as English as draught bitter, with its origins in the spectacular "cofyns" filled with boned birds inserted into each other in descending order of size, which were ushered in to music at medieval banquets.
The crust, which must be sturdy enough to stand alone (though moderns will cheat by using a cake tin with detachable base) is the means to an end, a hermetic container which allows the contents to be cooked long and slowly into a richly flavoured mass which may be eaten hot or cold, and cuts like a cake. It is not a dish to make on impulse, or in a hurry, but for an all-out celebration, it converts a selection of quite homely ingredients into a spectacular presentation which will be long remembered.
One large pie, its lid decorated with pastry acorns, oak leaves or rosettes, looks grander for a buffet table, but it may be more convenient to make two smaller pies and keep one by to eat later, cold. Raised pies keep well in a cool place.
You'll need a special raised pie mould with spring clips (or a pâté mould with hinged drop-down sides), or you can use a large, or two medium-sized, cake tins with removable base.

METRIC/IMPERIAL
STOCK
meat trimmings, bones, etc.
2 pig's trotters or sheep's
   feet
2 bay leaves
1 small glass port (optional)

HOT WATER CRUST
900 g/2 lb strong or plain
   flour
1½ tsp salt
350 g/12 oz lard, or 225 g/
   8 oz lard and 100 g/4 oz
   butter
300 ml/½ pint water
1 egg

FILLING
350 g/12 oz pork
   sausagemeat or minced
   belly pork
1 tbsp finely chopped fresh
   herbs such as sage, thyme
   or marjoram
1 tsp anchovy essence
   (optional)
100 g/4 oz unsmoked or
   mild-cure bacon or
   gammon, diced
1.5 kg/3–3½ lb boneless
   lean meat or game
salt and black pepper

Make the jelly stock first. Put all the ingredients into a pan with cold water to cover and bring to the boil, skimming off any grey scum. Simmer for 1½–2 hours, or till reduced to about half. Strain through a fine-meshed sieve lined with muslin/cheesecloth to catch impurities. Set aside.

To make the hot-water crust, warm the flour and 1 teaspoon salt in a large bowl in the oven at lowest setting. Heat the fat and water together till boiling and boil for 1 minute, then with care, pour the mixture into the flour, stirring vigorously till it coheres into a lump. As soon as it is cool enough to handle knead the paste vigorously, punching and rolling it till smooth. Leave to prove in a warm place while you prepare the ingredients for the filling.

Preheat the oven to moderate (180°C/350°F/Gas Mark 4).

Prepare the filling by mixing the sausagemeat or pork with the herbs, anchovy essence (if used) and diced bacon. Cut the meat into slivers, chunks or slices as appropriate, removing any skin, gristle, bone etc. Season with salt and pepper.

To shape the "cofyn", first lightly grease the tin or mould. Break off about one third of the warm paste for a lid, and put the remainder into the tin. Begin working it with a stretching, knuckling movement across the bottom and up the sides of the tin, working fast so that it does not become cool and crumbly. Roll out the reserved paste to make a lid.

Fill the paste-lined tin in layers, starting with sausagemeat, then pieces of meat or game, then sausagemeat again. Fill tightly, and dome the top slightly. Lay on the lid, dampen the edges and press to seal. Knock back the edges with a knife (see illustration), pierce a hole in the centre top for steam to escape, and use any pastry trimmings to model decorative leaves, acorns, etc for the lid. Brush over with an egg wash made by beating the egg with the remaining ½ teaspoon salt.

Put the pie, or pies, into the oven and bake for 1 hour, then turn the heat down one setting and bake for a further 1½ hours for smaller pies, 2½ hours for a large one. The pie is cooked when the

AMERICAN
STOCK
meat trimmings, bones, etc.
2 pig's feet
2 bay leaves
1 small glass port wine
   (optional)

HOT WATER CRUST
6½ cups bread or all-
   purpose flour
1½ tsp salt
¾ lb (3 sticks) lard, or ½ lb
   (2 sticks) lard and 1 stick
   butter
1¼ cups water
1 egg

FILLING
¾ lb bulk pork sausage or
   ground pork belly (sides)
1 tbsp finely chopped fresh
   herbs such as sage, thyme
   or marjoram
1 tsp anchovy extract, or
   anchovy paste to taste
   (optional)
¼ lb slab bacon or lightly
   smoked ham, diced
3–3½ lb boneless lean meat
   or game
salt and black pepper

juice shows no pinkness if a skewer is inserted through the steam hole. If the lid begins to brown too quickly during the long cooking, lay a piece of foil on top. When the pie is out of the oven, pour the heated stock through a funnel into the central hole, shaking to distribute it evenly.

Raised pies can be served hot, releasing the most appetizing aromas, but their full handsomeness is best seen when they are allowed to cool overnight, so the stock binds the filling into a glistening solid mass. Serve with baked potatoes, a strong leafy salad, English mustard and a rousing homemade chutney or pickle.

NB As with all ancient dishes there is no definitive recipe. Small individual pies, moulded around a jam jar, and filled up after cooking with melted gooseberry or redcurrant jelly, make dashing buffet or picnic food. A long pie, cooked in a loaf tin, can have hard-boiled eggs inserted into the filling, for a visual surprise. For extra lusciousness, diced foie gras or truffle peelings can be added judiciously. Boned game birds, stuffed with smaller birds (pheasant with quail inside, for instance) also look spectacular. But don't omit the forcemeat or the stock.

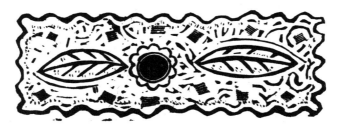

KIDNEY AND LEEK PUDDING

Even people who don't think they like kidneys enjoy this
steamed pudding. It is an economical supper or lunch dish,
full of flavour. The good thing about suet puddings is that you
can make and leave them, and a little overcooking won't
harm.

METRIC/IMPERIAL
4 lambs' kidneys, cored and
   chopped
225 g/8 oz trimmed leeks,
   sliced
1 cooking apple, peeled,
   cored and chopped
1 tbsp chopped fresh thyme,
   or 1 tsp dried thyme
Worcestershire sauce
salt and black pepper

SUET PASTRY
225 g/8 oz self-raising flour
½ tsp salt
50 g/2 oz fresh
   breadcrumbs
100 g/4 oz shredded suet
about 150 ml/¼ pint water

Grease a 900 ml–1.2 litre/1½–2 pint pudding
basin/1 quart steaming mold.

   Make the suet pastry (see page 21) and divide it
into 4 pieces. Lightly roll out one piece of pastry
and put in the bottom of the basin, to come a little
way up the sides. Put a third of the kidneys, leeks,
apple and thyme on top, and add a shake of
Worcestershire sauce and a little salt and pepper.
Lightly roll out the next piece of pastry, to fit the
bowl roughly. Put another layer of filling on.
Repeat, and cover with the last piece of pastry.

   Cover with greaseproof/wax paper and steam
for about 2½ hours. Serve with a salad or stir-fry
vegetables. Tzatziki (page 28) adds bite.

AMERICAN
4 lamb kidneys, cored and
   chopped
½ lb trimmed leeks, sliced
1 tart apple, peeled, cored
   and chopped
1 tbsp chopped fresh thyme,
   or 1 tsp dried thyme
Worcestershire sauce
salt and black pepper

SUET PASTRY
1¾ cups self-rising flour
½ tsp salt
1 cup fresh breadcrumbs
1 scant cup shredded beef
   suet
about ⅔ cup water

BEEF OLIVES

METRIC/IMPERIAL
450 g/1 lb lean braising
    steak, thinly sliced
3 tbsp fresh breadcrumbs
2 tsp chopped parsley
1 tsp chopped fresh thyme
a little grated lemon rind
salt and black pepper
milk to moisten
1 heaped tbsp flour
50 g/2 oz dripping or oil
1 onion, peeled and sliced
1 carrot, peeled and sliced
300 ml/½ pint water

Preheat the oven to moderate (180°C/350°F/Gas
Mark 4).

Cut the beef slices into pieces about 7.5 cm/3 in
square and flatten well with a rolling pin. Mix the
breadcrumbs, parsley, thyme, grated lemon rind,
and salt and pepper to taste together with just
enough milk to make them hold together. Put a
little on each square, roll up and fasten with string
or wooden sticks.

Dust the olives with half the flour and brown
them in the fat in a frying pan. Pack into a
casserole. Brown the vegetables and add to the
casserole.

Stir the rest of the flour into the juices in the
frying pan, season and add the water. Bring to the
boil, and pour over the meat. Cover with a lid and
cook for 1½ hours.

AMERICAN
1 lb lean beef top round
    steak, thinly sliced
3 tbsp fresh breadcrumbs
2 tsp chopped parsley
1 tsp chopped fresh thyme
a little grated lemon rind
salt and black pepper
milk to moisten
1 heaping tbsp flour
4 tbsp drippings or oil
1 onion, peeled and sliced
1 carrot, peeled and sliced
1¼ cups water

PUNCH-NEP

Nep comes from neep, which is an old Scots name for turnip.
Punch is one of those good old English words with about half
a dozen different meanings.
This is a simple dish, to be served piping hot. Good with
roast beef.

METRIC/IMPERIAL
450 g/1 lb potatoes, peeled
    and sliced
450 g/1 lb turnips, peeled
    and sliced
40 g/1½ oz butter
salt and black pepper
150 ml/¼ pint double
    cream

Boil or steam the vegetables separately until
tender. Mash them with the butter, and plenty of
salt and pepper, and mix them well together until
smooth.

Put in a hot dish and smooth the surface. Heat
the cream. Punch (or poke?) holes all over, well
down into the potato-turnip blend. Pour the cream
into the holes and serve.

AMERICAN
1 lb potatoes, peeled and
    sliced
1 lb turnips, peeled and
    sliced
3 tbsp butter
salt and black pepper
⅔ cup heavy cream

LEMON DAINTY

A traditional, very tasty and not rich pudding, this comes in many variations.

METRIC/IMPERIAL

grated rind and juice of 1
  lemon
25 g/1 oz butter
175 g/6 oz caster sugar
25 g/1 oz flour
200 ml/⅓ pint milk
2 eggs, separated

Preheat the oven to moderate (180°C/350°F/gas Mark 4).

Beat together the butter, sugar, flour, milk, lemon rind and juice and egg yolks, or blend in a food processor. Beat the egg whites stiffly and fold in.

Put in a greased soufflé dish, and stand in water in a baking dish. Bake for about 35 minutes or until risen and set.

Serve hot or cold, with cream, plain yogurt or crème fraîche.

AMERICAN

grated rind and juice of 1
  lemon
2 tbsp butter
¾ cup sugar
3 tbsp flour
1 scant cup milk
2 eggs, separated

APPLE PORTER CAKE

The most wonderfully moist and succulent cake, this can be served hot as a dessert, with cream. It keeps very well, too. (It must be started at least 6 hours before final cooking.)

METRIC/IMPERIAL

225 g/8 oz cooking apples,
  peeled, cored and finely
  chopped (prepared
  weight)
225 g/8 oz mixed dried fruit
175 g/6 oz light muscovado
  or demerara sugar
150 ml/¼ pint Guinness
350 g/12 oz self-raising
  flour
2 tsp mixed spice
175 g/6 oz butter, cut into
  pieces
1 egg, lightly beaten
1 tbsp demerara sugar for
  the top

Mix the apples with the dried fruit, sugar and Guinness in a bowl. Leave overnight.

Preheat the oven to moderate (160°C/325°F/Gas Mark 3). Grease and line the bottom of a 20 cm/ 8 in cake tin with greaseproof/wax paper.

Sift the flour and spice together into a large mixing bowl. Rub in the butter with your fingertips to make a fine breadcrumb consistency. Pour in the apple mixture and the egg and stir well. Turn into the tin and smooth the surface. Sprinkle the extra sugar over.

Bake for about 1¾ hours or until a skewer inserted in the centre comes out clean. Leave for a few minutes in the tin, and then turn out on to a wire rack to cool, or serve at once.

AMERICAN

2 cups peeled, cored and
  finely chopped tart apples
1⅓ cups mixed dried fruit
1 cup firmly packed light
  brown sugar
⅔ cup Guinness or other
  dark beer
2½ cups self-rising flour
2 tsp apple pie spice
1½ sticks butter, cut into
  pieces
1 egg, lightly beaten
1 tbsp light brown sugar for
  the top

LEMON SUGAR CAKE

Another plain and simple cake which everyone likes, because of its very fresh lemony taste, crunchy top and moist inside.

METRIC/IMPERIAL
grated rind and juice of 1
  lemon
100 g/4 oz butter or
  margarine
225 g/8 oz sugar
2 eggs
100 g/4 oz self-raising flour

Preheat the oven to moderate (180°C/350°F/Gas Mark 4).

Beat the butter or margarine with half the sugar until light and creamy. Beat in the eggs one at a time, adding a spoonful of flour with each. Fold in the rest of the flour and the grated lemon rind.

Put into a greased and floured cake tin and bake for about 40 minutes.

Turn the cake out on to a wire rack. Quickly mix together the lemon juice and remaining sugar. Pour over the cake, so that the juice runs in and the sugar remains as a crust on top. Leave to cool.

AMERICAN
grated rind and juice of 1
  lemon
1 stick butter or margarine
1 cup sugar
2 eggs
¾ cup self-rising flour

EGG NOG

A traditional British pudding, piled in glasses at Christmas time for wassailing.

METRIC/IMPERIAL
2 eggs, separated
2 tbsp sugar
4 tbsp brandy or rum
freshly grated nutmeg
300 ml/½ pint milk
25 g/1 oz shredded almonds
25 g/1 oz chopped
  crystallized lemon or
  mixed fruit
150 ml/¼ pint double
  cream

Put the egg yolks, 1 tablespoon sugar, 3 tablespoons brandy, and nutmeg to taste in a bowl. Heat the milk to boiling and pour over the egg mixture. Cook the custard over a pan of hot water, stirring, until it thickens. Add the almonds and crystallized fruit. Pour into glasses and leave to get cold.

Beat the egg whites with the remaining sugar until stiff. Whip the cream until thick. Fold the egg whites and remaining brandy into the cream. Pile on top of the custard. Serve chilled.

AMERICAN
2 eggs, separated
2 tbsp sugar
4 tbsp brandy or rum
freshly grated nutmeg
1¼ cups milk
¼ cup slivered almonds
3 tbsp chopped crystallized
  lemon or mixed fruit
⅔ cup heavy cream

SUMMER PUDDING

The fruit for this pudding must be dark-red in colour: blackcurrants, raspberries and redcurrants mixed, blackberries and apple, damsons or other plums, or a mixture of some or all of these. If using blackberries and apple, use more blackberries, say 450 g/1 lb to 225 g/8 oz of apple.

METRIC/IMPERIAL
about 675 g/1½ lb fruit
  (prepared weight)
50—75 g/2—3 oz sugar
sliced white bread

AMERICAN
about 1½ lb fruit (prepared
  weight)
¼—⅓ cup sugar
sliced white bread

Cook the fruit with the sugar, using more sugar for sour fruit such as damsons and blackcurrants. Taste to see they are sufficiently — but not too — sweet. Only use a little water for cooking, just enough to prevent the fruit and sugar sticking initially.

Remove the crusts from the bread slices. Cover the insides of a 1.2 litre/2 pint pudding basin/5 cup round domed mold with the slices cut to fit. Pour in the fruit and as much of its juice as you can, right to the brim. Cover with a layer of bread. Soak it with any remaining juice.

Stand the basin on a plate. Put a saucer or small plate on top of the pudding, and weigh it down. Leave overnight in a cold place.

Next day, slip a knife around the inside of the basin. Invert a plate over the top, turn over and give a sharp shake to turn the pudding out. Serve with any remaining juice, and whipped cream.

ALMOND CAKE

A deceptively simple cake, this is sophisticatedly plain, straightforward and tasty, in other words excellent with coffee or for a tea-party, or eaten as a dessert.

METRIC/IMPERIAL
50 g/2 oz ground almonds
100 g/4 oz butter or
    margarine
150 g/5 oz caster sugar
3 eggs, separated
½ tsp almond essence
50 g/2 oz self-raising flour

AMERICAN
½ cup ground almonds
1 stick butter or margarine
¾ cup sugar
3 eggs, separated
½ tsp almond extract
7 tbsp self-rising flour

Preheat the oven to moderate (180°C/350°F/Gas Mark 4).

Beat the fat and sugar together until creamy. (Soft margarine is the easiest to mix; butter tastes better.) Add the egg yolks one at a time, beating well in. Add the almond essence. Fold in the flour mixed with the ground almonds. Beat the egg whites until stiff, and fold in.

Line an 18 cm/7 in round cake tin with greased greaseproof/wax paper. Pour in the cake mixture and bake for 50 minutes to 1 hour. Test if the cake is done by inserting a skewer into the centre; it should come out clean.

OATCAKES

What gives oatcakes their special taste is the fat used. Ideally this should be beef dripping, but lard will do. Or use a mixture of lard and bacon fat. These must be made speedily, rolled while the mixture is warm, or they will crumble.

METRIC/IMPERIAL
175 g/6 oz fine oatmeal
50 g/2 oz flour
½ tsp salt
25 g/1 oz dripping or lard,
    melted
boiling water to mix

AMERICAN
2 cups fine oatmeal
7 tbsp flour
½ tsp salt
2 tbsp drippings or lard,
    melted
boiling water to mix

Preheat the oven to moderate (180°C/350°F/Gas Mark 4)

Mix the oatmeal, flour and salt together. Add the melted fat and enough boiling water to make a firm dough. Roll out very thinly and cut out circles about 7.5 cm/3 in diameter or triangles. Place on a baking sheet and bake for about 30 minutes or until the oatcakes have just turned light brown. Cool on a wire rack. Oatcakes keep well in an air-tight tin, and are excellent served with cheese and soups.

FOOD FOR FRIENDS

The mainspring of true hospitality is the civilized and generous belief that pleasures shared are pleasures multiplied. The sharing of food chosen and cooked by oneself symbolizes the sharing of deeper, lasting things: friendship, love, laughter, experiences. Few sounds are more gratifying than the happy roar of a company delighted by each other, the food, the setting, the charm of the moment. Presentation matters, but is most captivating when it seems natural and spontaneous. Most food looks more appetizing in either decorative pottery dishes, or the plainest white ones. Time and thought, directed with affection, have always counted for more than display and extravagance when feeding one's friends. We hope the recipes in this chapter will convince you that the game still is definitely worth the candle. And by the way, don't forget the candles, lots of them: they are cheap magic no one ever tires of.

ROUILLE, OR RED PEPPER SAUCE

This sauce is almost as delicious and tasty as pesto, and as versatile spooned into soups, or spooned over pasta. Serve it with fish or meat.

You can vary the hotness of the sauce by putting a larger or smaller amount of red chilli in. Chillies do vary in hotness (as well as size), so it's just as well to put in less than you might need at first, and then add more.

You can make this by hand using a mortar and pestle, but it is a cinch in a blender or food processor.

METRIC/IMPERIAL
1 red pepper
1 thick slice of bread
2 cloves garlic, peeled and crushed
fresh red chilli pepper to taste
2 tbsp olive oil
1 tbsp sunflower oil

Soak the bread in water. Grill/broil the pepper until black and soft, then peel, deseed and chop it. Squeeze the bread to remove excess water. Blend or mash the red pepper, garlic and bread together, with a little chopped fresh hot pepper. Add the oils gradually, then add a little water or stock if the sauce is too thick.

AMERICAN
1 sweet red pepper
1 thick slice of bread
2 cloves garlic, peeled and minced
fresh hot red chili pepper to taste
2 tbsp olive oil
1 tbsp sunflower oil

HOT GREEN BEAN AND MUSHROOM SALAD

Either fine or sliced large green beans are suitable for this.

METRIC/IMPERIAL
675 g/1½ lb green beans
225 g/8 oz button mushrooms, sliced
mustard vinaigrette dressing (see page 28)

Steam or boil the beans in a very little water until just barely cooked; drain and refresh with cold water.

Mix the beans and mushrooms with enough vinaigrette dressing to coat the vegetables while the beans are still warm. Eat this immediately, or leave the salad to cool before serving.

AMERICAN
1½ lb green beans
½ lb button mushrooms, sliced
mustard vinaigrette dressing (see page 28)

PATSY'S CHICKEN TERRINE

White, green and rosy pink, this is as pretty a terrine for a summer dinner party as one could hope to see, and it tastes absolutely delicious.

MAKES ABOUT 10 SLICES

METRIC/IMPERIAL
1.5 kg/3½ lb chicken
1 lime or lemon
1 onion, peeled
25 g/1 oz butter, cut into pieces
225 g/8 oz chicken livers, trimmed
2 bunches watercress, stalks removed
8 sprigs fresh tarragon
150 ml/¼ pint double cream
3 eggs
salt and black pepper
150 g/5 oz streaky bacon rashers
8 fresh spinach leaves, thick stalks removed

Preheat the oven to fairly hot (200°C/400°F/Gas Mark 6).

Squeeze the lime or lemon over the chicken. Place the onion and squeezed fruit inside the bird, dot with the butter and wrap in foil. Roast for 1 hour 20 minutes, basting occasionally. Leave to cool.

Gently fry the livers in a little of the chicken fat till browned but still pink inside. Leave to cool.

Remove the breast meat from the chicken and cut it into large chunks. Put aside. Remove the remaining meat from the carcass, discarding skin and bones.

Preheat the oven to moderate (160°C/325°F/Gas Mark 3).

Place the watercress leaves, tarragon leaves, cream, eggs and onion from the bird into a food processor. Add the chicken meat, except that from the breast, and process till smooth. Season with salt and pepper. Mix this with the breast meat and livers.

Line a 900 g/2 lb/9 × 5 × 3 inch loaf pan with bacon and pour in the mixture. Cover with buttered foil. Place the pan in a large roasting pan filled with enough hot water to reach halfway up the sides of the loaf pan. Bake for 2 hours. Cool completely. Blanch the spinach leaves in boiling water, and use to wrap the unmoulded terrine when cold.

AMERICAN
3½ lb chicken
1 lime or lemon
1 onion, peeled
2 tbsp butter, cut into pieces
½ lb chicken livers, trimmed
2 bunches watercress, stems removed
8 sprigs fresh tarragon
⅔ cup heavy cream
3 eggs
salt and black pepper
5 oz bacon slices
8 fresh spinach leaves, thick stems removed

ROMEO AND JULIET SALAD

This is rather a grand name for a distinctive salad made of very ordinary ingredients. It was invented by a chef in Verona. Its flavouring is rosemary and it is a salad to remember ("There's rosemary, that's for remembrance").

METRIC/IMPERIAL
approximately equal
    weights of:
waxy potatoes, such as
    Desirée
turnips, peeled
celery, chopped
2 tsp finely chopped fresh
    rosemary
2 or 3 tbsp olive oil
a good squeeze of lemon
    juice
salt and black pepper

Cook the potatoes, in their skins, and the peeled turnips in separate pans of boiling water. Cook both vegetables until just tender but still firm. Drain and leave to cool. Peel the potatoes and chop them; chop the turnips.

Chop the rosemary leaves very finely, as they are so pungent; it's quite shocking to bite a whole spike. About 2 teaspoons will probably be sufficient, but taste the salad after it has rested and the flavours have developed, to see if more is needed. Put the rosemary, olive oil, lemon juice and salt and pepper to taste into the salad bowl. (The dressing should be more oily than lemony.) Add all the vegetables, and toss well. Leave to get quite cold.

If liked, decorate this pale salad with chopped celery leaves. Another apposite decoration is one tomato rose placed in the centre. If you use this salad as part of a buffet meal, place it next to a red tomato salad, or Peperonata (see page 67).

Rosemary and love seem to be well-connected in several ways, which is why this herb is reported to be "useful in love-making", though we are not told how. Rosemary means "dew of the sea", and Venus, goddess of love, came out of the sea foam. A sprig of rosemary used to be worn at weddings. More down to earth, it's supposed to be good for flatulence and improving the memory.

AMERICAN
approximately equal
    weights of:
firm boiling potatoes
turnips, peeled
celery, chopped
2 tsp finely chopped fresh
    rosemary
2 or 3 tbsp olive oil
a good squeeze of lemon
    juice
salt and black pepper

CROSTINI

Crostini are slices of French bread, cut rather chunkily —
and at an angle to give more surface — with a savoury topping.
The slices can be fried, or covered and grilled/broiled, and
served hot or cold.
A typical Tuscan hors d'oeuvre is a couple of different
crostini, with a small slice of smoked ham or other sausage.

CROSTINI WITH GOAT'S CHEESE
Cut a French loaf in thick slanting slices. Spread
with butter, olive oil and crushed garlic. Put a slice
of goat cheese on each slice, and sprinkle rosemary
over. Grill/broil until the cheese melts.

CROSTINI WITH CHICKEN LIVERS
Chop up about 175 g/6 oz of chicken livers, dredge
with flour and cook gently in a little butter. Season
with salt, pepper, a squeeze of lemon and a little
sherry or fruit juice. Fry four slices of French bread
lightly in a mixture of oil and butter. Cover with the
livers.

CHEESE CROSTINI
Cut thick slanting slices from a French loaf. Trickle
olive oil over each slice, and cover with a thick slice
of Gruyère cheese. Lay slightly overlapping in an
oven dish, and bake for about 8 minutes in a fairly
hot oven (200°C/400°F/Gas Mark 6). Meanwhile,
chop up a small can of anchovies, and heat in their
oil with a little butter. As soon as they are hot, and
disintegrating, pour them over the crostini and
serve.

PRAWNS IN THEIR SHELLS
WITH AÏOLI

Crude food, but a delicious if messy start to a summer meal. The prawns must be sold in their shells, and large enough to make peeling not too fiddly. This quantity is not too much for 4 people, and the shellfish make a handsome sight piled up on a dish. If you want to be elegant you can give people their own small bowl of aïoli, a delicious garlic mayonnaise. Provide a large communal plate for the shells, napkins and finger bowls.

METRIC/IMPERIAL
675 g/1½ lb cooked fresh
  prawns in shell

AÏOLI
2 egg yolks
½ tsp dry mustard
3–4 large cloves garlic,
  peeled and crushed
300–450 ml/½–¾ pint
  fruity green olive oil
juice of 1 large lemon
salt and black pepper

AMERICAN
1½ lb cooked fresh shrimp
  in shell

AÏOLI
2 egg yolks
½ tsp dry mustard
3–4 large cloves garlic,
  peeled and minced
1¼–2 cups fruity green
  olive oil
juice of 1 large lemon
salt and black pepper

A mayonnaise made with 2 egg yolks is less likely to curdle than that made with a single yolk, especially if the eggs have been taken out of the refrigerator long enough before to come to room temperature. Beat the yolks in a bowl with a wooden spoon, adding the mustard and garlic. (Whacking the peeled garlic cloves with a cleaver and then chopping them to a mush with a pinch of salt takes longer than using a garlic crusher but is said to release a finer flavour.) Start adding the oil a drop at a time, beating steadily; pouring the oil from a small jug helps to control the flow. For a minute or two the outcome will be in doubt, but suddenly, all being well, the mixture will cohere and stiffen. At this point the oil can be added in larger gouts, beating each time till smooth. The mixture will go on becoming denser as more oil is added. By the time you have beaten in the minimum quantity of oil given, the mayonnaise should have reached the proper consistency – a stiff, shiny, yellow emulsion; it will absorb more oil if you wish. Squeeze in the lemon juice, beat and taste: the mayonnaise should be a little sharp. Add salt and pepper judiciously.

A bowlful of aïoli will be more than you need, so decant the excess into a bowl and run a film of oil on top to keep it usable.

SMOKED SALMON
TARTLETS

Use smoked salmon off-cuts or trimmings for this recipe. There are various ways of finding them — either in supermarkets, wrapped, or in fish shops, where they sometimes sell off all the little scrappy bits, and slightly bony pieces, rolled up in half a salmon skin. If you see them for sale, and you've got a freezer, it's worth snatching them, sorting out all the best pieces, and keeping them for future use. They are also sold in bags, frozen and nameless, and these can be disappointing — mostly the tough dark scrapings next to the skin. So it's always wise to see exactly what you are buying. There can be as much as 225 g/8 oz or more very usable salmon in one portion.

This will seem like a weird way of making pastry, without rolling or cutting, but it makes just the right very thin, crisp and dry pastry case to hold its shape well cold. If you are making a lot of pastry for a party, with covered pies or patties and other shapes, then you will be using a more orthodox pastry, and rolling it out. In that case cut out circles for the tartlets as usual.

This will make about 15 small tarts.

METRIC/IMPERIAL
100 g/4 oz flour
a pinch of salt
50 g/2 oz softened butter or soft margarine
about 2 tbsp water

SMOKED SALMON FILLING
100 g/4 oz smoked salmon, finely chopped
a little lemon juice
2 small eggs
120 ml/4 fl oz single cream, or 100 g/4 oz low-fat soft cheese
2 dashes of Angostura bitters
½ small onion, peeled and grated
black pepper

AMERICAN
¾ cup + 1 tbsp flour
a pinch of salt
4 tbsp softened butter or soft margarine
about 2 tbsp water

SMOKED SALMON FILLING
¼ lb smoked salmon, finely chopped
a little lemon juice
2 small eggs
½ cup heavy cream or low-fat soft cheese
2 dashes of Angostura bitters
½ small onion, peeled and grated
black pepper

Preheat the oven to moderately hot (190°C/375°F/Gas Mark 5). Have ready 15 or 16 small tartlet tins (or trays of 9 and 6). Grease them well, right up to the rim.

To make the pastry, put the flour and salt into a bowl and lightly mix in the soft fat with your fingers. Sprinkle on the water and mix around with a knife, then form into a dough with your hands. (Scrape back into the bowl any dough on your fingertips.)

Break off 15 or 16 little pieces of dough, depending on how many tartlet tins you have. Make each piece roughly into a ball shape, put it in a tin and with your fingertips, press it out to cover the bottom of the tin and up the sides. Don't worry if the top edge is smooth, or if the pastry looks uneven. It's amazing how cooking will even it all out, and a slightly uneven rim looks authentically professional, funnily enough.

To make the filling, distribute the smoked salmon among the pastry cases. Squeeze lemon juice over each. Beat the eggs with the cream, and add the bitters, onion and black pepper to taste. Pour into the pastry cases, filling them right up to the very brim. Put to bake for 30 minutes.

Leave the tartlets to cool for a minute or two, then turn them out onto a wire rack and leave to cool completely.

This pastry is also useful for fruit tartlets or making small quiches.

Using butter for the pastry and cream in the filling is obviously rich; margarine and low-fat soft cheese make a much less calorific version, and with such a strong-tasting filling it's really hard to tell the difference. Interesting to experiment with both.

RAW BEEF WITH GREEN PEPPERCORNS

After many tastings and experiments this seems to me one of the most delicious ways of serving raw meat, which is as tender as the best smoked salmon. It means marinating the meat for 2 or 3 hours.

If you get to the butcher's first thing in the morning, his meat should still be firm from keeping in the cold store overnight. Ask him to slice the steak as finely as he can on his meat slicer. Or give him warning and he will probably do it for you when the meat is right for cutting.

METRIC/IMPERIAL
225 g/8 oz sirloin steak, cut into wafer-thin slices

MARINADE
1 tbsp green peppercorns, crushed
1 tbsp lemon juice
3 tbsp olive oil
1 tsp Dijon mustard

AMERICAN
½ lb boneless sirloin steak, cut into wafer-thin slices

MARINADE
1 tbsp green peppercorns, crushed
1 tbsp lemon juice
3 tbsp olive oil
1 tsp Dijon-style mustard

Mix the marinade ingredients together. Pour over the meat and leave to marinate for 2 or 3 hours.

Serve the meat just as it is, or with salsa verde, as a first course.

If you want to slice the meat yourself, freeze it for half an hour or so, then take it out and slice it as thinly as you can using a sharp knife. Really, though, it's best to have the butcher do the job.

POTATOES IN WINE

METRIC/IMPERIAL
450 g/1 lb potatoes, peeled and sliced
2 onions, peeled and sliced
40 g/1½ oz butter
1 bay leaf
salt and black pepper
½ bottle dry white wine

AMERICAN
1 lb potatoes, peeled and sliced
2 onions, peeled and sliced
3 tbsp butter
1 bay leaf
salt and black pepper
½ bottle dry white wine

Sauté the onions in the butter in a frying pan until softened. Add the potato slices with the bay leaf and salt and pepper to taste. Pour over the wine to cover the vegetables, then simmer gently, covered, for 1 hour. Add more wine during the cooking if necessary to prevent sticking.

Transfer the vegetables to a serving dish using a slotted spoon. Boil the cooking liquid to reduce it a little, then pour over the vegetables and serve.

LEEKS VINAIGRETTE

Such an appetizing starter, one kicks oneself for not thinking
of it more often.

METRIC/IMPERIAL
450 g/1 lb small young
  leeks, trimmed
1 hard-boiled egg, shelled
  and yolk and white
  separated
3 tbsp red wine vinegar
6 tbsp fruity olive oil
1 shallot, or 2 spring onions,
  peeled and finely
  chopped
salt and black pepper
pinch of sugar or mustard
  powder (optional)

If you have a steamer use this to cook the leeks
because it ensures they cook without becoming
mushy. Otherwise, boil in a covered pan with 1 cm/
½ inch of water till just tender (test with a fork).

Meanwhile, make the vinaigrette. Mash the egg
yolk and stir in the vinegar, oil, shallot and salt and
pepper to taste. A pinch of sugar or mustard
powder can be added for a change.

Lay the leeks on a serving dish and pour over the
vinaigrette. Sprinkle over chopped egg white,
refrigerate and serve very cold.

AMERICAN
1 lb small young leeks,
  trimmed
1 hard-boiled egg, shelled
  and yolk and white
  separated
3 tbsp red wine vinegar
6 tbsp fruity olive oil
1 shallot, or 2 scallions,
  peeled and finely
  chopped
salt and black pepper
pinch of sugar or mustard
  powder (optional)

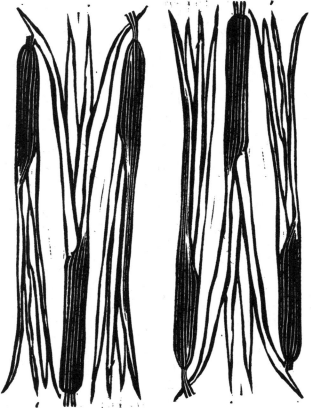

INDONESIAN MINCED PORK

What chefs cook off duty is interesting in much the same way as seeing how designers furnish their own homes. Michel Roux and his wife cook tasty but unpretentious dishes, like this savoury stir-fried meat mixture scooped up in lettuce leaves, when they have friends round for a meal. It's fun to cook and fun to eat, and a pointer to everyone else who likes to see and feed friends without too much ceremony, after a long day's work.

METRIC/IMPERIAL

675 g/1½ lb fatty pork
    (leaner belly or middle
    neck), minced
6–8 dried Chinese
    mushrooms
2 tsp cooking oil
1 tsp sesame oil
a small knob of fresh ginger,
    peeled and grated
3 cloves garlic, peeled and
    crushed
about 100 g/4 oz canned
    bamboo shoots, drained
    and cut into small dice
about 100 g/4 oz canned
    water chestnuts, drained
1 tbsp oyster sauce
1 tbsp light soy sauce
½ tsp five spice powder
black pepper

TO SERVE

1 crisp Webb's or cos lettuce
bunch of spring onions,
    trimmed and halved
    lengthwise

AMERICAN

1½ lb fatty pork (leaner side
    pork or shoulder), ground
6–8 dried Chinese
    mushrooms
2 tsp cooking oil
1 tsp sesame oil
a small piece of fresh ginger
    root, peeled and grated
3 cloves garlic, peeled and
    crushed
about ¼ lb canned bamboo
    shoots, drained and cut
    into small dice
about ¼ lb canned water
    chestnuts, drained
1 tbsp oyster sauce
1 tbsp light soy sauce
½ tsp five spice powder
black pepper

TO SERVE

1 head iceberg or romaine
    lettuce
bunch of scallions, trimmed
    and halved lengthwise

Put the Chinese mushrooms to soak in a little warm water for 20 minutes. Separate the lettuce leaves, wash and dry them, then put in the bottom of the refrigerator to crisp. Slice the spring onions lengthways into two. Put them in a covered bowl in the refrigerator.

Heat the two oils in a wok, or large frying pan, and fry the garlic and ginger for a few seconds over moderate heat to flavour the oil. Put in the pork, increase the heat and fry, stirring and turning and breaking up lumps, till browned. Add the bamboo shoots, water chestnuts, drained Chinese mushrooms, oyster and soy sauces, five spice powder and pepper to taste. Stir well till thoroughly mixed, and cook for a minute or 2 longer till most of the liquid has evaporated.

Turn the mixture into a round, hot bowl. This goes in the middle of the table where everyone can reach. People spoon some of the pork mixture on to a lettuce leaf, add a couple of pieces of onion, roll up and eat in their fingers. Serve something fishy with this, such as a Malaysian fish soup, or prawn balls, and maybe a vegetable stir-fry or an interesting salad.

ORANGE FISH PIE

This is a particularly good amalgam of tastes.

METRIC/IMPERIAL
675–900 g/1½–2 lb white
  fish fillets (cod, haddock
  or coley)
a little milk
1 bay leaf
1 large sprig parsley
grated rind and juice of 1
  large orange
salt and black pepper
50 g/2 oz fresh
  breadcrumbs
1 clove garlic, peeled and
  finely chopped
75 g/3 oz butter

Preheat the oven to moderately hot (190°C/375°F/
Gas Mark 5).
  Poach the fish gently in a little milk and water
with the herbs until it is opaque and cooked.
  Carefully drain the fish and remove all skin and
bones without breaking up the flesh too much. Put
the fish in an ovenproof dish (to serve from) and
pour over the orange juice. Season with a little salt
and pepper.
  Mix the breadcrumbs with the orange rind and
garlic. Fry in the butter, and scatter over the fish.
Bake until the breadcrumbs are crisp.

AMERICAN
1½–2 lb white fish fillets
  (cod, haddock or pollock)
a little milk
1 bay leaf
1 large sprig parsley
grated rind and juice of 1
  large orange
salt and black pepper
1 cup fresh breadcrumbs
1 clove garlic, peeled and
  finely chopped
6 tbsp butter

PORK ROLL WITH CHICKEN AND HAM

This is very good either hot or cold, and useful sliced for a buffet.

METRIC/IMPERIAL
1 pork fillet
1 chicken breast, skinned
  and boned
2 tbsp green peppercorns,
  crushed
2 tbsp chopped parsley
50-g/2-oz can anchovy
  fillets, drained and
  chopped
1 large slice cooked ham
a little butter

Preheat the oven to cool (150°C/300°F/Gas
Mark 2).
  Cut open the pork lengthways, like a book, and
beat it out flat. Similarly slice open the chicken
breast, and flatten. Mix the peppercorns with the
parsley and chopped anchovies.
  Lay out the pork and spread a little of the
peppercorn mixture over. Cover with the ham,
then more mixture, the chicken, and the remaining
mixture. Roll it up along its length, tie with string
and put in a baking dish. Dot with a little butter
and roast for about 2 hours.

AMERICAN
1 pork tenderloin
1 chicken breast half,
  skinned and boned
2 tbsp green peppercorns,
  crushed
2 tbsp chopped parsley
2-oz can anchovy fillets,
  drained and chopped
1 large slice cooked ham
a little butter

GRAVAD TROUT

Gravad Lax is raw salmon marinated in sugar, salt and dill; Gravad Stromming is raw herring similarly done. Not knowing the Swedish word for trout, and as it does not appear to be much used, we compromise here and call this recipe Gravad Trout, hoping the Swedes will forgive. This method gives the fish a texture a bit like smoked salmon, and yet not quite, with a vastly different taste. But it preserves the delicate pink flesh colour. It's well worth trying, now that trout is farmed, and therefore cheaper.

METRIC/IMPERIAL
2 pink-fleshed trout, filleted
2 tbsp sunflower oil
2 tbsp lemon juice
1 tsp Dijon mustard
2 tsp sugar
2 tsp salt
black pepper
fresh dill leaves, or 1 tsp
  dried dill

AMERICAN
2 pink-fleshed trout, filleted
2 tbsp sunflower oil
2 tbsp lemon juice
1 tsp Dijon-style mustard
2 tsp sugar
2 tsp salt
black pepper
fresh dill leaves, or 1 tsp
  dried dill

To fillet the trout yourself, simply cut off the head, and slice the flesh away from the backbone.

Mix all the other ingredients together, except for the fresh dill. Spread a quarter of the mixture, pressing it in, on to one fillet. Lay some dill leaves on top. (If you have not got fresh dill, then the dried will be mixed in with the dressing.) Place another fillet on top, with more mixture, and so on. Finally put a plate on top, and put the fish in the refrigerator. It's a good idea to pile the fish in a soup dish, because the juices will run out a little.

Let it marinate for 12 to 24 hours. Turn the fish and pour the juices over once in a while, if you happen to be around, but it's not essential.

To serve, slice the fish as thinly as possible, as for smoked salmon. It may not come very properly in slices, probably more in small pieces. Pour over a little of the oily, lemony juice, and give a pepper grind over it.

Slice the skin into thin strips, about 1 cm/½ in wide, and fry until brown and crisp. Serve with the fish, accompanied by brown bread and butter.

As the fish will probably come away in flakes rather than large slices, serve them with cocktail sticks, to pick up a mouthful-size piece with.

MOULES MacCORMAC

This excellent dish began life as moules marinières with knobs on, acquired an Asian fillip under the tutelage of cookery writer Daramjit Singh plus modifications suggested by an exceptional mussel broth in Edinburgh, and was then surprised to find its twin in a medieval dish described in Dorothy Hartley's *Food in England*. Whatever its pedigree, it is always worth waiting for.

METRIC/IMPERIAL
900 g/2 lb fresh mussels
50 g/2 oz butter
450 g/1 lb onions, peeled and chopped
2 large leeks, trimmed and chopped
2 cloves garlic, peeled and chopped
1 cm/½ inch cube fresh ginger, peeled and chopped
120 ml/4 fl oz water
1 tsp turmeric, or ½ tsp saffron threads
pinch of cayenne pepper
salt and black pepper
300 ml/½ pint dry white wine
200 ml/⅓ pint cream (optional)
small handfuls of fresh parsley or coriander, finely chopped

Put the mussels in clean water and scrub them well. Pull and scrape off the beard and any barnacles with a small stout knife. Any mussels that are not tightly closed, or feel unusually heavy (which can mean a shell full of mud), should be discarded. Leave the mussels in cold water while you prepare the vegetable base for the soup.

Melt the butter in a large heavy pan with a lid and soften the onions and leeks over moderate heat, with the lid half on. Add the garlic and ginger and leave to simmer, without browning.

Put the mussels and water in a large pan over a high flame and shake and turn them with a wooden spoon till all are open – 1–2 minutes. Remove immediately. (Discard any mussels that remain stubbornly closed.) The mussels should be just firm enough to remove from shells. Using a slotted spoon, lift the mussels out onto a large dish and cool slightly.

Pour the mussel pan liquid through a fine sieve, to remove any grit, directly into the vegetable pan. Add the turmeric or saffron, cayenne and black pepper to taste. Simmer very gently, covered.

Remove the mussels from their shells (some people might prefer to leave them on the half shell). They should be added all at once, with the wine, to the oniony stock. Replace the lid and leave to barely simmer for a further 3–5 minutes.

Add the cream and parsley, and serve in shallow soup plates with lots of hot bread.

AMERICAN
2 lb fresh mussels
4 tbsp butter
1 lb onions, peeled and chopped
2 large leeks, trimmed and chopped
2 cloves garlic, peeled and chopped
½ inch cube fresh ginger root, peeled and chopped
½ cup water
1 tsp turmeric, or ½ tsp saffron threads
pinch of cayenne
salt and black pepper
1¼ cups dry white wine
1 cup cream (optional)
small handful of fresh parsley or coriander (cilantro), finely chopped

PEARS IN WHITE WINE AND GINGER SAUCE

METRIC/IMPERIAL
4 pears, peeled
200 g/7 oz white sugar
250 ml/8 fl oz white wine
pared rind and juice of ½
lemon
2 tbsp peeled fresh ginger
cut into very fine
matchstick strips
250 ml/8 fl oz whipping or
double cream

Put 1 tablespoon of sugar to one side. Put the remaining sugar, the wine, lemon rind and ginger in a large pan and heat, stirring to dissolve the sugar. When the mixture boils, add the pears. Turn down the heat and simmer the pears until tender, about 15–20 minutes. Leave to cool.

Put the pears in a serving bowl. Discard the lemon rind from the syrup and boil to reduce it until quite thick. Remove the ginger and set aside. Pour the syrup over the pears, and sprinkle the ginger on top.

Whip the cream with the reserved sugar and a little lemon juice. Serve with the pears.

AMERICAN
4 pears, peeled
1 cup white sugar
1 cup white wine
pared rind and juice of ½
lemon
2 tbsp peeled fresh ginger
root cut into very fine
matchstick strips
1 cup heavy cream

CHOCOLATE DELIGHT

This is a more luxurious version of a chocolate summer pudding. You need a large serving bowl. Chill the dessert for several hours in the refrigerator before serving.

SERVES ABOUT 8

METRIC/IMPERIAL
225 g/8 oz dark cooking
chocolate
4 tbsp water
4 tbsp icing sugar
4 eggs, separated
1 tsp vanilla essence
225 g/8 oz sponge finger
biscuits
100 g/4 oz shelled pecans or
walnuts, chopped
300 ml/½ pint whipping
cream, whipped

Break up the chocolate and melt it over a gentle heat with the water. Remove from the heat. Add the sugar and mix well. Beat the egg yolks, and add to chocolate mixture with the vanilla. Whisk the egg whites until stiff and fold them in.

Put a layer of fingers in the bowl, then cover with the chocolate mixture. Add a sprinkling of chopped nuts and a few spoonfuls of whipped cream. Repeat the process, using up all the ingredients, and finishing with a topping of cream.

Chill well, and serve from the dish.

AMERICAN
8 squares semisweet
chocolate
4 tbsp water
¼ cup confectioners' sugar
4 eggs, separated
1 tsp vanilla extract
½ lb ladyfingers
1 cup chopped pecans or
walnuts
1¼ cups heavy cream,
whipped

MERINGUES

A jar or tin full of little meringues is an insurance against all unexpected visitors or sudden cravings for something sweet — an instant dessert, filled with plain or sweetened whipped cream, with chopped walnuts or fresh fruit added.

METRIC/IMPERIAL
for each egg white:
pinch of salt
50 g/2 oz caster sugar
a little vanilla essence

AMERICAN
for each egg white:
pinch of salt
¼ cup sugar
a little vanilla extract

Preheat the oven to very cool (110°C/225°F/Gas Mark ¼).

Beat the egg white stiffly with the salt. Add half the sugar, and beat until the mixture forms peaks. Fold in the vanilla and the rest of the sugar. Put on an oiled baking sheet in teaspoonfuls (or larger spoon if you wish), or pipe with a forcing bag.

Put in the oven and leave to dry out for about 1½ hours. Turn the oven off, and let the meringues remain inside until they are dry and quite hard to the touch.

Serve joined together in pairs.

GINGER SYLLABUB

METRIC/IMPERIAL
100 ml/3½ fl oz ginger wine
grated rind and juice of 1
  small lemon
50 g/2 oz white sugar
2 tbsp brandy
300 ml/½ pint double
  cream
4 ginger biscuits (optional)
a little finely chopped stem
  ginger

Gently warm the ginger wine, lemon rind and juice and sugar in a saucepan until the sugar dissolves. Allow to get cold, then stir in the brandy.

Whip the cream until very thick. Stir in the ginger wine mixture.

Put ginger biscuits in the bottom of four ramekins or wineglasses. Spoon the syllabub on top. Decorate with the stemmed ginger. Chill and serve very cold.

AMERICAN
½ cup ginger wine
grated rind and juice of 1
  small lemon
¼ cup white sugar
2 tbsp brandy
1¼ cups heavy cream
4 ginger snap cookies
  (optional)
a little finely chopped stem
  ginger

APPLE CHARLOTTE

A fine, traditional pudding based on the simplest of ingredients, this is excellent when properly done. The important thing is to cook the apples slowly and gently to a thick, dryish purée.

METRIC/IMPERIAL
900 g/2 lb dessert apples,
  peeled, cored and sliced
grated rind of ½ lemon
½ tsp ground cinnamon
115 g/4 oz sugar
5–6 slices day-old bread,
  crusts removed
115 g/4 oz unsalted butter,
  melted

Put the apples to cook over the lowest possible heat with the lemon rind and cinnamon, covered, till soft. If they show signs of sticking, add a couple of tablespoons of water. Process or sieve to make a thick purée. Return to the heat, add the sugar and stir till dissolved.

Preheat the oven to moderate (180°C/350°F/Gas Mark 4).

Cut the bread into fingers and triangles to fit the inside of an ovenproof pudding bowl or deep round mould, and to make a lid. Dip the pieces in melted butter and line the bowl with them. Fill with the apple purée and cover with bread. Bake for about 40 minutes, or till the bread is crisp and golden brown.

Serve hot or warm, with a jug of cold cream.

AMERICAN
2 lb sweet apples, peeled,
  cored and sliced
grated rind of ½ lemon
½ tsp ground cinnamon
½ cup sugar
5–6 slices day-old bread,
  crusts removed
1 stick unsalted butter,
  melted

TRIMMINGS AND TOUCHES

The more I cook, and eat, the more I find myself warming to the optional extras in the kitchen — the home-made jams or pickles, the batch of oatcakes warm from the oven, the oils and vinegars pungent with herbs and spices. In all these old kitchen processes that transmute one substance into another, one touches on the mystery of power as the old alchemists pursued it. This is not to say that the bits and pieces in this chapter are not useful, too. Home-made goodies almost always taste better than the bought variety while costing infinitely less. True there is some work involved in preparing and cooking the recipes in this chapter, but by the time the moment comes to serve them, the effort is subsumed in a glow of achievement which is almost as pleasant as the taste and texture of your own culinary creation.

PICKLED GRAPES

Delicious condiments like these are worth the extra effort because they lift simple dishes into a different class. Eat these with cheese, or cold meat, or cream cheese. Use small cheap grapes, at the height of the season, or home grown ones which have not properly ripened. Give a jar as a present.

The recipe comes from *From garden to kitchen* by Douglas Bartrum, one of those fastidiously greedy books which deserve to be better known.

METRIC/IMPERIAL
900 g/2 lb grapes, washed and destalked
300 ml/½ pint white wine vinegar
600 ml/1 pint water
225 g/8 oz sugar
1 small cinnamon stick
4 tsp cloves
4 allspice berries

Pack the grapes into sterilized jars. Boil the remaining ingredients for a few minutes. Let cool, then pour over the grapes. Seal the jars and store in a cool place. Leave for a month or two before eating.

AMERICAN
2 lb grapes, washed and destalked
1¼ cups white wine vinegar
2½ cups water
1 heaping cup sugar
1 small cinnamon stick
4 tsp cloves
4 tsp allspice berries

PLUM, ORANGE AND WALNUT PRESERVE

This preserve is wonderful in little tarts, or added to apple pies or puddings, or just spread on bread.

METRIC/IMPERIAL
675 g/1½ lb plums such as Victoria or greengage, stoned and stones reserved
2 whole oranges, chopped
1.35 kg/3 lb sugar
225 g/8 oz shelled walnuts, chopped

Put the stones from the plums in a muslin, cheesecloth or J-cloth bag. Simmer the plums, oranges, bag of stones and sugar, with just enough water in the bottom of the pan to stop the fruit burning, for about 1 hour. Remove the stones.

Add the walnuts and cook for a further 30 minutes.

Put in dry warm jars, and cover tightly.

AMERICAN
1½ lb plums such as El Dorado or greengage, pitted and pits reserved
2 whole oranges, chopped
3 lb (about 7 cups) sugar
2 cups chopped walnuts

SPICED LEMON PICKLE

That pre-eminent restaurant, The Carved Angel in Dartmouth, England, serves this extraordinary pickle with chicken croquettes, but it also adds zest to cold meats and curries. Tom Jaine, formerly of The Carved Angel, gives the recipe in his absorbing book, *Cooking in the Country*. Buy a box of lemons wholesale, and make a year's supply, because it is amazingly good.

METRIC/IMPERIAL
900 g/2 lb lemons
450 g/1 lb onions,
600 ml/1 pint wine vinegar
675 g/1½ lb granulated
   sugar
25 g/1 oz salt
50 g/2 oz green ginger
2 large fresh green chillies
1 tbsp whole allspice
1 dsp whole cardamom
1 dsp whole coriander

Bag up the three spices in a muslin. Peel and grate the ginger. Deseed the chillies and chop finely. Squeeze the lemons and slice them thinly. Peel the onions and slice them as well. Mix the onion and lemon slices in a large bowl with the lemon juice, the vinegar, the chillies, green ginger and spices. Allow to steep overnight.

The next day, cook everything gently for about one and a half hours until the lemon skins are really tender. Once the sugar is added they will soften no more. Add the sugar, stir until dissolved and boil briskly for twenty minutes. Use a wide and solid saucepan. Pot up in jars with vinegar-proof lids and leave for at least a month before eating. It will keep almost indefinitely.

   Recipe © Tom Jaine 1986 from *Cooking in the Country* published by Chatto & Windus Ltd 1986.

AMERICAN
2 lb lemons
1 lb onions
2½ cups wine vinegar
1½ lb (about 3½ cups)
   sugar
1½ tbsp salt
2 oz fresh ginger root
2 fresh hot green chili
   peppers
1 tbsp allspice berries
2 tsp cardamom pods
2 tsp coriander seeds

DAMSON CHEESE

Shining, and almost black, an old-fashioned damson cheese is one of the most royal of treats, served up at the end of a meal with a selection of nuts and cheeses, or as a relish with cold meats, or simply spread on crusty bread.

METRIC/IMPERIAL
2.25 kg/5 lb damsons
300 ml/½ pint water
sugar
1 cinnamon stick (optional)

AMERICAN
5 lb damson plums
1¼ cups water
sugar
1 cinnamon stick (optional)

It is quicker to stone the fruit after cooking. Put the washed damsons and water into a large pan, cover and simmer gently over low heat till soft, shaking and stirring occasionally. Turn into a large strong sieve, a batch at a time, and push the mixture through with a wooden spoon into a weighed bowl. Discard stones and skins which refuse to go through. Weigh the resulting pulp.

Measure out 350 g/12 oz/1¾ cups sugar to every 450 g/1 lb of pulp. Warm the sugar in a low oven for a few minutes while you reheat the fruit pulp with the cinnamon stick if used. Add the warm sugar to the pulp and stir till dissolved, then continue cooking and stirring over low heat till the mixture is dryish, and a spoon pressed down on top leaves a mark.

Fish out the cinnamon stick. Spoon the fruit cheese into oiled glass or pottery dishes; cover with wax paper and then with foil. Store in a dark, dry place for 2–3 months, or longer (it keeps well) before eating, sliced into thin slices or chunks.

✎ The same treatment can be given to quinces or apples, or a mixture of both, remembering that the proportion of sugar to fruit pulp is a constant.

SPICED KUMQUAT PRESERVE

METRIC/IMPERIAL
450 g/1 lb kumquats
450 g/1 lb sugar
600 ml/1 pint water
5 cm/2 inch cinnamon stick
6 cloves

Pierce the kumquats several times with a fork. Cover with water, bring to the boil and boil for a minute or so, then drain and set aside.

Dissolve the sugar in the measured water, with the cinnamon and cloves. Bring to the boil and cook for 10 minutes. Add the fruit and cook until it is shiny and tender. Put in jars, and cover tightly. Leave to mature for a month before use.

AMERICAN
1 lb kumquats
2¼ cups sugar
2½ cups water
2 inch cinnamon stick
6 cloves

MARROW OR PUMPKIN CHUTNEY

Chutneys provide a good way of using up a surplus of cheap vegetables, as well as giving a somewhat tasteless main ingredient a lot of borrowed flavours.

METRIC/IMPERIAL
2.5 kg/5 lb marrow or pumpkin, peeled, seeded and cut into 2 cm/¾ inch cubes
900 g/2 lb tomatoes, peeled and chopped
450 g/1 lb onions, peeled and sliced
8 cloves garlic, peeled and chopped
1.5 kg/3 lb soft brown sugar
175 g/6 oz sultanas
4 tbsp salt
1 tbsp black peppercorns
1 tbsp allspice berries
2.5 cm/1 inch cube fresh ginger, peeled and crushed
1 litre/1¾ pints white wine vinegar

Put all the ingredients into a large non-reactive pan. Bring slowly to the boil, stirring to dissolve the sugar, then cook gently for about 1½ hours, partly covered, till the mixture is soft but not too dry.

Ladle into warmed clean jars and cover with cling film or special jam covers before screwing on the lids (vinegar should not come into contact with metal). Store for a month of two to give the chutney time to mature. Eat with cold meats, cheese, curries, etc.

AMERICAN
5 lb pumpkin, peeled, seeded and cut into ¾ inch cubes
2 lb tomatoes, peeled and chopped
1 lb onions, peeled and sliced
8 cloves garlic, peeled and chopped
3 lb (about 9½ cups) brown sugar
1 heaping cup golden raisins
¼ cup salt
1 tbsp black peppercorns
1 tbsp allspice berries
1 inch cube fresh ginger root, peeled and crushed
1 quart white wine vinegar

BRAMBLE JELLY

Making blackberries into jelly solves the pip problem, and
gives one of the most evocative of all preserves, delicious with
hot scones or soda bread.

METRIC/IMPERIAL
1.75 kg/4 lb blackberries
450 ml/¾ pint water
sugar
grated rind and juice of 2
    lemons

Simmer the blackberries with the water till soft,
then push through a fine sieve, pressing to extract
the last drop of juice. Measure the juice, and weigh
out 450 g/1 lb/2¼ cups sugar to each 600 ml/
1 pint/2½ cups juice.

   Put the juice, sugar, lemon juice and a little
grated rind into a pan, bring to the boil and boil till
the jelly reaches setting point.

   Pot into warmed jars, seal with wax paper
(dipped in brandy if you like) and cover.

AMERICAN
4 lb blackberries
2 cups water
sugar
grated rind and juice of 2
    lemons

ELDERFLOWER
CHAMPAGNE

This is the most extraordinary drink — why it goes bubbly
without any added yeast (and why occasionally it doesn't!), I
don't quite know. Anyway, with any luck, you will get a
light, flowery, bubbly liquid which will keep for months.
Some people drink it after 14 days, but I prefer to keep it for
a couple of months before imbibing.

METRIC/IMPERIAL
3–4 elderflower heads in
    full bloom
pared rind and juice of 1
    lemon
4.5 litres/1 gallon water
675 g/1½ lb sugar
2 tbsp white vinegar

Cut the lemon rind into several pieces, and put
with the other ingredients into a large container.
Stir well, and steep for 24 hours. Strain and bottle.
Keep for at least 14 days before drinking.

AMERICAN
3–4 elderflower heads in
    full bloom
pared rind and juice of 1
    lemon
4½ gallons water
3⅓ cups sugar
2 tbsp white vinegar

SLOE GIN

It's a real shame that one can't make gin out of sloes — but even though one must buy the gin ready-made, the making of sloe gin is a ritual and a pleasure — and a test. Sloes are the fruit of the blackthorn, which, confusingly, is covered with fine small white flowers in the spring. Blackthorn bushes are unremarkable, and the small purple fruit hide among the leaves. Look for blackthorn on clay soil, where it grows most readily, among overgrown hedges.

METRIC/IMPERIAL
600 ml/1 pint sloes
900 g/2 lb demerara sugar
about 1 litre/1¾ pints gin

AMERICAN
2½ cups sloes
4 cups firmly packed light
  brown sugar
about 1 quart gin

Wash the fruit and pick the stalks off. Prick each fruit once or twice with a fork, and put with the sugar into a big bottle (an old cider bottle is ideal), with plenty of space to spare for the gin. Pour in the gin: there should be twice as much gin as fruit.

Now the ritual is to shake the bottle once each day, vigorously. Place it somewhere, on the landing for instance, where you will see it every day. The pleasure is to see the juice turning a deep red-purple. And the test is to wait for 14 weeks — or say from when you first picked the sloes in the autumn, until Christmas — when you can strain off the sloe gin and drink it.

I have not yet found a good use for leftover sloes. Despite their immersion in sugar all those weeks, they remain bitter enough to make your tongue curl.

🌿 Here is a sloe gin cocktail, to spin the precious stuff out a little: a *sloe gin rickey*. Mix a generous portion of sloe gin with a little crushed ice and a good squeeze of lime juice, and top up with soda water.

QUINCE JELLY

Quince trees are unpredictable — sometimes they fruit, sometimes they don't, but when they do, they bear a very odd, half apple- half pear-shaped thing, turning from green to yellow, and covered with a white furry dust. Quinces are to be found in the shops, if you're lucky, in late autumn. They are hard, no good to eat raw, but make a most beautiful, unique jelly.

It is preferable to use rather unripe fruit, which jells best. If the quinces are very orangey yellow and slightly soft, add some cooking apples. The more apples you add, the more you dilute the particular quince taste. The proportions suggested here make a good compromise.

METRIC/IMPERIAL
1.35 kg/3 lb quinces
450 g/1 lb Bramley cooking apples, chopped with peel and core
about 900 g/2 lb sugar
pared rind and juice of 1 lemon

AMERICAN
3 lb quinces
1 lb tart baking apples, chopped with peel and core
about 4½ cups sugar
pared rind and juice of 1 lemon

Wash the quinces and cut out any bad parts. Chop up without peeling, and put in a pan with the apples and just enough water to cover the fruit. Simmer until the fruit is turned to pulp.

Tip into a jelly cloth, if you have one, and leave to drip above a bowl overnight. You can rig up a good bag from muslin or cheesecloth, or use a J-cloth. Pull a kitchen drawer out a little way, and suspend the bag from the handle.

Measure the juice in the bowl: to each 600 ml/ 1 pint/2½ cups use 450 g/1 lb/2¼ cups sugar. Put the juice and sugar in a large pan with the lemon rind and juice. Stir over a gentle heat until the sugar dissolves, then boil fast.

After about 10 minutes, put a little jelly on a saucer, to test if it has reached setting point: as you draw a finger over it the surface should wrinkle.

Skim off any white scum, and pot in small, warmed jars. A fancy item is to put a little twist of the lemon peel in the top of each jar.

It's worth keeping any elegant small jars, from chutney or mustard, for instance, for bottling home-made jellies. They are rather special and make welcome presents.

🌿 Redcurrant and quince are the two best jellies, I think, to make to serve with meat and ham. Crab-apple is another good one, and is made in the same way as quince. Redcurrant jelly is made more or less the same, except that as the fruit is already soft and watery, you do not add so much water at first, or need to cook it so long. Add just a little water to the fruit, and cook on a low heat until the fruit is very soft. Drain overnight. Next day, add 550 g/1¼ lb/2¾ cups of sugar to each 600 ml/ 1 pint/2½ cups of juice. Dissolve the sugar slowly, and then boil fast. This should set quite quickly, so test after about 5 minutes.

🌿 Gooseberry mint jelly is excellent with cold meat and fish. Cover gooseberries with water, add a handful of mint, and cook until the fruit is soft. Drain, and add 450 g/1 lb/2¼ cups of sugar per 600 ml/1 pint/2½ cups of juice, then proceed as with the other jellies.

YOGURT CHEESE SPREADS OR THICK DIPS

Any of the following can be used to enliven the smooth, sharp tasting paste which results from draining yogurt overnight.

BASIL, GARLIC AND GREEN PEPPERCORN SPREAD

METRIC/IMPERIAL
550 g/1¼ lb plain whole
    milk yogurt, drained for 8
    hours
1 tbsp shredded fresh basil
1 clove garlic, peeled and
    crushed
1 tsp green peppercorns,
    crushed
½ tsp salt

Process or mash the ingredients into the yogurt cheese to mix thoroughly. Cover and chill for a couple of hours to allow the flavours to develop.

AMERICAN
1¼ lb (2½ cups) plain
    whole milk yogurt,
    drained for 8 hours
1 tbsp shredded fresh basil
1 clove garlic, peeled and
    minced
1 tsp green peppercorns,
    crushed
½ tsp salt

CORIANDER AND GREEN GINGER SPREAD

METRIC/IMPERIAL
450 g/1 lb plain whole milk
    yogurt, drained for 8
    hours
1 tbsp finely chopped fresh
    coriander
½ tsp finely grated fresh
    ginger
1 tsp turmeric
1 tsp lemon or lime juice
salt and black pepper

Mix all the ingredients with the yogurt cheese. Cover and chill before serving.

AMERICAN
1 lb (2 cups) plain whole
    milk yogurt, drained for 8
    hours
1 tbsp finely chopped fresh
    coriander (cilantro)
½ tsp finely grated fresh
    ginger root
1 tsp turmeric
1 tsp lemon or lime juice
salt and black pepper

CREAMY FRESH HERB AND GARLIC DIP

METRIC/IMPERIAL
550 g/1¼ lb plain whole milk yogurt, drained for 3 hours
1 tbsp very finely chopped fresh parsley
1 tbsp very finely chopped fresh herbs such as thyme, tarragon, basil or dill
1 large clove garlic, peeled and crushed
1 tbsp finely chopped chives or spring onions
salt and black pepper

For a soft, but not fluid dip, combine all the ingredients. For speed, the roughly chopped ingredients can be placed with the yogurt in a food processor and blended till smooth, Chill, and serve with crudités, strips of hot pitta bread or crackers.

AMERICAN
1¼ lb (2½ cups) plain whole milk yogurt, drained for 3 hours
1 tbsp very finely chopped fresh parsley
1 tbsp very finely chopped fresh herbs such as thyme, tarragon, basil or dill
1 large clove garlic, peeled and minced
1 tbsp finely chopped chives or scallions
salt and black pepper

SHRIKAND

METRIC/IMPERIAL
550 g/1¼ lb plain whole milk yogurt, drained for 3 hours
4 saffron threads, or ½ tsp powdered saffron
2 tsp warm milk
2–3 tbsp caster sugar
seeds from 4–5 cardamom pods, crushed to a powder
5 pistachio nuts, shelled and crushed into crumbs

Infuse the saffron in the milk for 1 hour. Add the saffron milk and sugar to the drained yogurt and process or whisk thoroughly to blend. Mix the cardamom seeds into the thick yellow cream, then stir in the crushed pistachios. Spoon into serving glasses or little dishes, and refrigerate till needed.

AMERICAN
1¼ lb (2½ cups) plain whole milk yogurt, drained for 3 hours
4 saffron threads, or ½ tsp powdered saffron
2 tsp warm milk
2–3 tsp sugar
seeds from 4–5 cardamom pods, crushed to a powder
5 pistachio nuts, shelled and crushed into crumbs

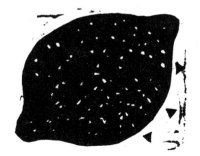

FLAVOURED OILS AND VINEGARS

It is absurdly simple to add flavour and fragrance to oils and vinegars by steeping herbs, spices and other ingredients in them, and the few minutes thought it takes will make a gratifying difference to your meals. Use flavoured oils for frying meat or fish, scented vinegars in stews and sauces, and use both in various combinations for concocting lively salad dressings. Any good-quality oil will benefit, but a wine vinegar is preferable to malt.

Flavoured vinegars are made in the same way as flavoured oils, but the infusing is best done in a warm or sunny place.

Bearing in mind that the vinegars are mainly used in salad dressings, you may find herbs are the most suitable flavouring.

BASIL OIL

Precious herbs like basil give enough of their essential pungency to allow you to enjoy the summery smell and taste right through winter, and this is a good use for the last leaves on your plants. A handful of basil leaves, stripped off the stalks and shredded with your fingers (better than chopping for basil) will give 600 ml/1 pint/2½ cups of oil a fine fragrance.

The same procedure can be followed with any other pungent herbs – thyme, savory, oregano or tarragon. There are no precise rules as to quantities: use more than the single sprig found in commercial bottles, but not so many that there is no room for the oil. Strip leaves off the stalks, and make sure they are all quite dry before inserting into clean, dry bottles and pouring in the oil.

CHILLI OIL

To each 600 ml/1 pint/2½ cups of oil (your normal frying oil is better for this than olive oil), add between two and five dried red chillies, bruised rather than broken up. This will add quite a punch to fried meat or fish or savoury fritters; go cautiously till you know what fire power you are dealing with.

GARLIC OIL

Add 6 peeled, lightly crushed garlic cloves to each 600 ml/1 pint/2½ cups of oil. Cap or cork the bottle, and leave, shaking occasionally, for a week or two before using.

MOCK OLIVE OIL

Looking about for a way of preserving surplus olives bought in a pack, I stuffed them into a jam jar and topped it up with corn oil. When I tasted the oil a week or two later I found it had picked up a distinct olive flavour. If you like to keep olives around, this is a neat way of getting them to work for you, flavouring a tasteless oil, while they wait to be eaten. Olives packed in brine should be dried with kitchen paper before being packed into a jar and covered completely with oil. I find the same trick helpful in boosting the flavour of one of the over-refined olive oils. Adding herbs, crushed garlic, chillies and so forth will flavour the olives as well as the oil.

FRUIT-FLAVOURED VINEGARS

Blackcurrants, raspberries and blackberries will all add colour and flavour to vinegar. Use dry fruit, picking out any mildewed ones, stalks and other debris, and allow about 450 g/1 lb to 600 ml/ 1 pint/2½ cups of vinegar. Leave the fruit in the vinegar for a week or two in a sunny place, then strain off into new bottles. These vinegars make stylish additions to gravies and sauces for chicken, duck and other meats, but use them lightly.

GINGER AND LEMON VINEGAR

Add a small cube of peeled, bruised fresh ginger root and a thin curl of lemon peel, scraped clean of white pith, to a bottle of white wine vinegar.

LAVENDER VINEGAR

Add 2–3 flowering lavender heads, picked on a hot day so they are quite dry, to a bottle of white wine vinegar, and leave to steep on a sunny windowsill for a week or two. Strain off and re-bottle.

STAR ANISE VINEGAR

A handy and cheap way of introducing some of that compulsive aniseed bouquet into a vinegar which can be added to fish sauces as well as salad dressings. Bruise 3–4 segments of one anise star (obtainable from Chinese grocers) and infuse in white or red wine vinegar for a few weeks before straining off.

THYME VINEGAR

Pack whole sprigs of flowering thyme into white or red wine vinegar and infuse for 2 weeks before straining off.

DRIED MUSHROOMS

Freshly picked wild mushrooms are the best for drying, but even the cultivated variety develop a much more intense flavour when dried. They can then be added to stews and other dishes, for their dark meaty pungency.

Wipe mushrooms clean, trim stalks and spread out on a sheet of foil in the bottom of the oven. Leave at the lowest setting, with the oven door just ajar, till the mushrooms are shrivelled and quite dry. Store in a covered jar.

HOME-MADE MUSTARD

Black, brown and white mustard seeds are obtainable from some delicatessens and speciality food shops and most oriental grocers, Indian ones especially. You can have fun making up your own mixtures, adding honey, brandy, apple juice or garlic to the basic paste made from powdered and whole seeds plus wine vinegar. Adding some whole seeds to a base of powdered ones gives the grainy texture popular in so many fashionable mustards.

To make one good sized jar, pound 115 g/4 oz of brown mustard seed to a powder in a mortar. Add 2 tablespoons of whole seeds, and then enough white or red wine vinegar, or cider vinegar, to bring it to the right consistency – about 300 ml/½ pint/ 1¼ cups. This base can now be modified to suit your taste with any of the ingredients listed above, or other combinations of spices that take your fancy. If you want it hotter still, experiment with grated horseradish or chilli powder. Store made mustard, covered, in a cool place.

DECORATIVE TOUCHES

Use these pretty garnishes and trimmings to raise ordinary plain food unpretentiously into another class.

TOMATO ROSES WITH WATERCRESS LEAVES

You need a really sharp or serrated little pointed knife for this, then it's easy as pie. Use firm tomatoes. Start peeling the tomato from the stalk end, very thinly, like an apple, winding your way in a strip not more than about 1 cm/½ in wide, to the end. Now roll up the peel again, starting from the end you finished with, and hey presto, an extraordinarily lifelike rose. To make it even more so, choose a good-looking stalk of watercress, with a couple of leaf-stalks, and arrange it as the stem and leaves of the rose. (The peeled tomato can now be sliced for a tomato salad, or used in cooking.)

JULIENNE STRIPS

Julienne strips are finely pared rind, or vegetables, cut into matchstick size. Blanch them, i.e. put in boiling water for a minute or two before using. Orange and lemon rind, carrots, peppers, both red and green, and turnips can all be used. Slivers of red cabbage are pretty too.

LEMON, ORANGE AND CUCUMBER TWISTS
Cut thin slices, then cut once from the edge to the centre, and twist.

VEGETABLE SHAVINGS
Not a very elegant name, but it gives the idea. Shave carrots, courgettes/zucchini, or any hard vegetable into long thin strips with a potato peeler. The shavings will curl and flow very prettily. These can be used purely as decoration, or, combined with a little dressing and chopped herbs will make a decorative small bowl per person of salad.

CUCUMBER NESTS
Cut cucumber into rounds 2.5—4 cm/1—1½ inches thick. Take out the seeds to make a hollow centre, then cook gently until translucent and soft in a little salted water. These nests can be filled and served either hot or cold. Fill with a cluster of peas, asparagus tips or scrambled egg. Cucumber nests can make an appetizer, filled with smoked salmon pieces, or mackerel, or prawns in a little mayonnaise and cream.

MELBA TOAST
Remove the crusts from a loaf of bread and slice the loaf thinly. Toast the slices, and while still warm, cut each slice into two thinner slices through the middle. Put the slices to get crisp in a moderate oven (180°C/350°F/Gas Mark 4). They will curl up, and a heap of curled melbas is an appetizing sight.

INDEX